ROOT-TO-STALK
COOKING

ROOT TO STALK COOKING

The Art of Using the Whole Vegetable

TARA DUGGAN

PHOTOGRAPHY BY CLAY MCLACHLAN

TEN SPEED PRESS
Berkeley

CONTENTS

Introduction 1

ROOTS 17
BEETS • TURNIPS • RADISHES • CARROTS • POTATOES

BULBS & STEMS 45
ASPARAGUS • CELERY • FENNEL • LEEKS

LEAVES 77
CABBAGE • CHARD • KALE • HERBS •
ROMAINE LETTUCE

FLOWERS 121
ARTICHOKES • SQUASH BLOSSOMS • BROCCOLI •
CAULIFLOWER

SEEDS 143
CORN • FAVA BEANS • PEAS

FRUIT 159
APPLES • AVOCADOS • BUTTERNUT SQUASH • CITRUS •
TOMATOES • WATERMELON

Recipes by Type 193
Acknowledgments 195
About the Author 197
Index 198

INTRODUCTION

We live in an era of vegetable obsessiveness. After several postwar decades when the only vegetables we knew were frozen or canned, we have awakened to a new age in which markets are overgrown with forests of leafy greens, emerald stalks, and columns of butterscotch-colored winter squash. We buy them up, wanting to cook food that is healthy, fresh, and natural. We even plant a garden or join a farm's Community Supported Agriculture (CSA) program to guarantee a basket of produce each week. Then we make a soup or stir-fry and find ourselves surrounded by extra leaves, stalks, and seeds, the flotsam and jetsam of a produce lover's cooking life.

We want to stay the course, but buying all this produce is starting to add up, and isn't it wasteful if you don't use it all? Those bags of pretrimmed broccoli florets seem to produce less waste, at least that we can see. But we want more flavor, more color, more nutrition, more life than they can offer. We want to embrace the whole vegetable.

This book will show you how to waste less, discover new depths of flavor, and save a little money by thinking differently about the produce you buy or grow. With these recipes, you can use more of those broccoli stalks, fennel fronds, artichoke leaves, and even carrot tops. The book tackles some common fruits, too, and it takes a similar thrifty approach to a few pantry staples to partner with them. My goal is both to help you use the fruits and vegetables you already love and to learn how to prepare ones that you may be less familiar with.

The recipes in this book are not all vegetarian, but they are all plant-based, the buzz word for a style of eating that puts vegetables, grains, and fruit at the center of the plate, with meat and fish revolving around like moons. Meat and fish traditionally play that supporting role in a number of cuisines, including Chinese and Italian, and the recipes here take inspiration from those countries, with dishes like Leek Greens Stir-Fry with Salty Pork Belly, which pairs a small amount of pork with the dark green part of the leeks most recipes tell you to throw out. I examine dozens of different vegetables and fruits, focusing on produce that tends to create the most waste, and give their extra parts—those roots, stems, leaves, and seeds—a chance to take their rightful place in the center of our diet.

Some of the ingredients used here, like carrot tops and beet greens, don't last very long once you remove them, so you really need to cook them first or at the same time that you use the main vegetable. If you don't have the time to prepare the greens within a day or two of taking them home, they might just end up in the compost bin, no questions asked. But if you are inspired to cook them, you will get another dish out of the deal, such as a carrot top salsa verde to drizzle over roasted root vegetables, when all you thought you were getting was carrots.

In some cases, your experimentation might lead you to rediscover why we don't eat certain vegetable parts. For example, I had little success turning corn silk into something anyone would want to eat, and my attempts at basil stem oil lead nowhere (it turns out they are grassy and bitter).

Tomato skins have more potential, but saving them is probably more trouble than it's worth. After setting aside the skins of a couple pounds of summer-ripe tomatoes I had used in a sauce, I dehydrated them in the oven for two hours and then ground them up in a food processor. In the end, I had a couple of tablespoons of very flavorful powder for all my trouble. In large amounts, it could be worthwhile, but for general daily use, it wasn't very useful.

Most of the time, however, using the vegetable parts most home cooks throw away is worth the effort. We can learn a lot about the subject from restaurant kitchens, where whole vegetable cooking is second nature because wasted food hurts the bottom line. But there is another reason chefs do it: flavor. Using different parts of the same

vegetable in various ways, such as the inner and outer stalks of celery, or the fennel fronds as well as the fennel, adds layers of nuance to a dish, since different parts of a plant are more intensely flavored, or differently flavored, than others. I hope that this book helps you become excited about all of the different possibilities waiting inside each vegetable.

Vegetables: The Passion and the Reality

I first got really into food, and vegetables, during several years my parents were stationed with the military in Naples, Italy. My brother, Ben, and I were in college in the United States, but we spent as much time in Italy as we could, drinking *cappucci*, as they call the milky espresso drinks there, and eating out with my parents while working summer jobs. In addition to sampling the region's amazing seafood, pizza, and pasta, we got to experience a whole new world of vegetables in unexplored preparations.

In *Naples at Table*, Arthur Schwartz writes that the Neapolitans were once called *mangiafoglie*, or "leaf eaters," because of their love of vegetables, which are grown in the fertile volcanic soil and sunshine the region is known for. I think of Californians as modern-day *mangiafoglie*, though in our case the leaves might refer to lettuce, since we eat salads at every opportunity. California's Salinas Valley is called the nation's salad bowl, and the state is responsible for growing much of the country's other vegetables and fruits. While California can boast having the largest number of farmers' markets in the country, the increased interest in fresh produce is a trend seen across the United States, where the number of farmers' markets grew by 40 percent between 2002 and 2012.

My own love of vegetables grew when I became a staff food writer for the *San Francisco Chronicle*, where I've had the opportunity to interview countless chefs and farmers who share a passion—sometimes extreme—for vegetables. But at the same time that I'm a farmers' market junkie and chronicler of obscure heirloom varieties of produce, I also wear other hats. For over a decade, I wrote a *Chronicle* column called "The Working Cook," where I created recipes that could be prepared in around thirty minutes. I made sure that the recipes always included fresh vegetables, but I struggled with the fact that plant-focused meals take a lot longer to prepare than meat or fish entrées. Whereas a chicken breast or pork chop does fine with a sprinkle of salt and a little time under the broiler, there is a lot more washing, peeling, and trimming that has to happen with vegetarian main courses. Plus there's the planning that goes into shopping and using up fresh vegetables before they go bad.

I'm also the mother of two young girls and, as I'm sure you'll find it shocking to hear, my children do not quite share my enthusiasm for vegetables. My ten-year-old, Dahlia, explained that she will like more vegetables when she gets older and loses more of her taste buds (unfortunately for her, that theory has been debunked). That means we usually have two or three vegetable dishes on the table at every dinner, with wilted broccoli raab for us among bowls of steamed green beans for them.

But I've realized that the more practical side of me—the harried mother and the quick recipe specialist—doesn't have to be at war with my inner *mangiafoglie*. I've learned to pair vegetables that require longer preparation with those that don't: corn that needs to be shucked and then cut off the cob is perfect with tomatoes, which only need to be chopped. Rather than laboriously peel winter squash, I might split it, roast it until soft, and then scoop out the caramelized flesh. Or I'll just leave it unpeeled, slice it, and roast it at high heat so that the skin becomes crispy and good to eat.

After all, many of these recipes were inspired by simple necessity, like when I had a ton of lemongrass from a big bunch I picked up at the farmers' market and a chicken that needed cooking. That night Lemongrass Grilled Chicken (page 109) was born. Hopefully recipes such as these will provide you with ideas when you have random ingredients but aren't sure what to make for dinner.

There is also hope for my girls, who love to help at their aunt and uncle's vegetable garden and in the kitchen, where they can be counted on to peel fava beans and shuck corn. And Elsie, my youngest, eats crunchy salads and artichoke leaves with abandon and seems to hold promise as a budding *mangiafoglie*.

Peels and Pesticides

In conventional farming, more pesticides reside on the skin of fruits and vegetables than inside, so when you are eating the peels, it's helpful to be aware of which types of produce tend to contain more of these chemicals. Each year the Environmental Working Group recognizes what it calls the Dirty Dozen, the types of produce that have been shown to have the most pesticide residue, even after washing, according to USDA testing. If you're concerned about pesticides, these are the vegetables and fruits you'll want to buy organic.

THE DIRTY DOZEN, PLUS TWO:

Vegetables:
- bell peppers
- celery
- cucumbers
- green beans
- kale or other greens
- lettuce
- potatoes
- spinach

Fruits:
- apples
- domestic blueberries
- grapes
- imported nectarines
- peaches
- strawberries

Conversely, the Environmental Working Group has found the following vegetables and fruit, which it calls the Clean 15, to be among the lowest in pesticide residue:

THE CLEAN 15:

Vegetables:
- asparagus
- cabbage
- corn
- eggplant
- mushrooms
- onions
- sweet peas
- sweet potatoes

Fruits:
- avocado
- domestic cantaloupe
- grapefruit
- kiwi
- mangoes
- pineapples
- watermelon

Source: Environmental Working Group *2012 Shopper's Guide to Pesticides in Produce*

Waste Not

Beyond the home economics benefits of whole-vegetable cooking, it also helps reduce your ecologic footprint. Estimates vary, but some experts say that as much as 40 percent of all food produced worldwide is wasted. Although many of the sources of waste are on the production and distribution end, there are plenty of things home cooks can do to save food, as Jonathan Bloom describes in his book *American Wasteland*. He writes that, according to USDA research, almost one-third of the vegetables in supermarkets, restaurants, and homes go to waste. And, according to a three-decade study called the Garbage Project by the University of Arizona, American households throw out 25 percent of their groceries overall.

Preventing herbs from turning to sludge in your refrigerator drawer will not end world hunger, but it can save you a dollar or two at a time—adding up to thousands of dollars per year for a family of four—and it will contribute overall to reducing food waste. By using more parts of the vegetables and fruits we eat, our overall consumption goes down. If we use carrot tops as an herb rather than buy a bunch of parsley, or cook beet greens rather than pick up a bunch of chard, that's one less plant that has to be watered, fertilized, harvested, transported, and refrigerated, not to mention one less thing to buy.

Just as foraging for wild blackberries or growing your own tomatoes helps you to appreciate your food more, learning creative uses for the underutilized parts of vegetables and fruits makes you more aware of small things you can do to prevent waste. If you frequent farmers' markets, are a member of a CSA, or grow your own vegetables, you will have even more opportunities to make use of the tips and recipes in this book.

Vegetable Scraps Stock

When conversation comes around to how to use up extra vegetable parts, the first thing people bring up is stock. So let's just get this out of the way, why don't we? Some cooks go so far as to keep vegetable peelings and bits of chopped onion or carrots in their freezer. I'm not quite that organized and tend to use up scraps as I have them, with the exception of asparagus stalks, which I put in the freezer every time I trim asparagus until I reach a critical mass (see Asparagus Stalk Stock, page 47).

Whether you're a scrap hoarder or more the spontaneous type, here's a way to figure out how much and what kinds of—and parts of—vegetables to use when making stock for soups and sauces.

AMOUNTS AND METHOD

For every quart (4 cups) of water, use roughly 3 cups of scraps plus some herbs. For 2 quarts of water, then, you should have about 5 or 6 cups of chopped vegetables or scraps. If you don't have enough scraps to make the amount of stock you want, add some chopped onion, carrots, and celery.

Place everything in a big pot, bring to a simmer, and then cook gently for 30 to 40 minutes before straining and cooling the stock. The stock will keep, refrigerated, for several days and freezes well for a couple months.

The final quantity of stock will be about two-thirds the volume of the water you start with. That means if you start with 2 quarts of water, you'll end up with about 5 cups of stock.

WHAT TO USE

Use a mix of vegetables from each column, using a small amount from the Earthy and Deep group to add depth to vegetable stocks.

Sweet
- carrot peels
- corn cobs
- fennel fronds, cores, and stalks
- garlic ends or whole cloves, peeled
- leeks, white and green parts
- lettuce spines and outer leaves
- onion ends
- pea pods
- tomato ends, peels, seeds

Bitter and/or Vegetal
- asparagus stems and peels
- carrot tops (use sparingly)
- celery leaves, ends, and trimmings
- chard and kale stalks
- cucumber peels
- fava pods
- green bean ends
- leek greens
- potato skins
- zucchini peels or trimmings

Earthy and Deep
- bay leaves
- dried mushrooms
- dried tomatoes
- herb stems and trimmings: Italian parsley, cilantro, thyme, oregano
- kombu (Japanese dried seaweed)
- mushroom stems
- peppercorns
- Parmesan cheese rinds (not a vegetable, but definitely a scrap!)
- tomato paste

WHAT NOT TO USE

Avoid using artichoke parts or leaves (too bitter), beet parts and leaves (they can turn the stock pink), and cruciferous vegetables such as cauliflower, broccoli, and brussels sprouts, which will give the stock a cabbage-y flavor.

Anatomy of a Vegetable

LEAVES

STEM

ROOT

BULB

ROOT-TO-STALK
COOKING

How the Book Is Organized

The book is divided botanically into six chapters representing different edible parts of a plant, including the roots, stems, leaves, flowers, seeds, and fruit (including many fruits we treat as vegetables). Since asparagus is a shoot, it's in the "Stems" chapter, and artichokes and cauliflower are in the "Flowers" chapter. Once you become familiar with the basic botany, it's easier to discover how many more parts of each vegetable—broccoli leaves, fennel stalks, and apple cores, for instance—might be turned into something delicious.

Although most of the recipes focus on the edible parts of plants we often ignore, others provide ideas about how to use up certain kinds of produce, like herbs and fruit, that you may often have an excess of. For example, I give you ideas for quick sauces and marinades to make with all the herbs you might have left from making other recipes.

While some recipes in this book use both the actual vegetable plus the extra parts, such as the Carrot Slaw with Greek Yogurt, Lemon & Coriander (page 31), which combines shredded carrots with peppery chopped carrot tops, others use just the scraps, such as the Potato Skin–Bacon Fat Chips (page 38). Throughout the book, look for notes with recipes that use just a portion of the vegetable, which will direct you to recipes that use the other parts.

1

ROOTS

At first, I was hesitant to start a book with roots and tubers, the wallflowers of the vegetable world. They aren't popular like volleyball team captain Tomato, and they aren't serious and sexy like class president Asparagus. But just as Silicon Valley has shown us that geeks can be cool, so too have farmers' markets turned roots and tubers into something special. They aren't always pretty—think of the ugly dangling roots of celeriac, which have to be trimmed before you find the gorgeous ivory vegetable underneath. And with the exception of beets and carrots, most come in muted colors, blanched from spending too much time underground. Their thick skins can be hard to penetrate, but they are full of nutrients and sweet carbohydrates—after all, the roots provide food for the rest of the plant—and they are grounded by complex, earthy nuances. They roast beautifully, creating a side dish that can go with almost any meal. You may be used to thinking of roots and tubers as background players, but they are dependable and true, like that loyal friend from drama club you never took to the prom.

Season: Most of these vegetables are available year round, but springtime is when you are most likely to find specialty varieties and the young roots with their greens attached. New potatoes, which are young uncured potatoes, arrive in the spring, too.

Beet Greens Salad with Whole Grains, Pickled Beets & Fresh Cheese 20

Beet Greens Strata 23

Braised Turnips & Greens with Soy Butter 26

Radish Leaf Salad with Corn, Tomatoes & Salted Cucumbers 29

Carrot Slaw with Greek Yogurt, Lemon & Coriander 31

Carrot Top Salsa Verde with Roasted Root Vegetables 34

Quinoa-Carrot Tabbouleh 36

Potato Skin–Bacon Fat Chips 38

Scraps Latkes 40

Beets, Turnips, and Radishes

If you buy beets, turnips, or radishes at a farmers' market or health food store, they usually come with their beautiful greens attached. I consider them an extra gift, yet I often see people lopping the greens off right at the market; after all, they take up a lot of room. Supermarkets usually get rid of the greens, in part for that reason and in part because the vegetables store better without them since they draw out moisture. But when the greens are bright and unwilted, you know the vegetable was just plucked from the earth.

Dark green and red-veined, beet greens have a flavor and texture that is similar to that of their close cousin, chard. Radish and turnip greens, on the other hand, are smaller, the color of grass, and peppery. You can sauté any of them as you would chard or kale (see page 87), or, if they are fairly young and tender, you can use them in salads. If you're not sure, just take a bite and make sure they taste good raw.

To store these vegetables, remove the tops from beets, turnips, and radishes and store them, unwashed, in a plastic bag in the refrigerator. Greens and tops will keep for 2 days, radishes and baby turnips for 1 week, and beets and mature turnips for several weeks.

Prep Tip

Beets, turnips, radishes, and their greens all need to be washed well before cooking or the final dish will be gritty. Remove the roots, then scrub the vegetables and soak the leaves in a large bowl of water. Lift the leaves out of the dirty water, and refresh the water until you see no sand in the bottom of the bowl.

BEET GREENS SALAD WITH WHOLE GRAINS, PICKLED BEETS & FRESH CHEESE SERVES 4 TO 6 AS A SIDE

Pickled beets

1 bunch beets, scrubbed and trimmed (halved if large)

Kosher salt

½ cup sherry vinegar or red wine vinegar

1¼ cups uncooked whole-grain bulgur, quinoa, wheat berries, and/or farro

Salad

Greens from 1 bunch beets, washed (see Prep Tip, page 18)

¼ cup plus 1 teaspoon extra-virgin olive oil

2 cloves garlic, finely chopped

2 green onions, white and green parts, thinly sliced

1 tablespoon chopped fresh thyme, rosemary, or a mix of herbs

4 teaspoons sherry vinegar or red wine vinegar

½ teaspoon kosher salt

⅛ teaspoon freshly ground pepper

½ cup crumbled fresh goat or feta cheese

½ cup toasted walnut halves

Both beets and beet greens are important elements of this salad, which also includes cooked whole grains with fresh herbs, olive oil, and vinegar. I like to use a mixture of grains for a combination of textures and flavors, which is also a good way to use up small amounts of grains in your pantry. Start with a big pot of salted boiling water, then add the one that takes the longest—wheat berries often win that award—and add the others at intervals so that they each cook according to their suggested cooking times. This salad can be prepared 2 days in advance.

Note: Bunches of beets can vary in size. This recipe works well with three or four medium beets and their greens. If you'd like a salad with more greens or your beets didn't come with tops, use chard instead.

....

Preheat the oven to 400°F.

To make the pickled beets, place the beets in a baking dish just large enough to hold them in a single layer. Season with salt and add enough water to cover the bottom of the pan by ½ inch, then cover tightly with foil and roast until tender when pierced with a knife, 40 minutes to 1 hour depending on their size. Remove from the pan, let cool, then peel, wearing gloves if you want to avoid staining your hands. Cut the beets into wedges and place them in a small bowl. Add enough to vinegar to almost cover the beets and toss to coat. Let marinate in the refrigerator, stirring occasionally, until they taste somewhat pickled, at least 30 minutes and up to 4 hours. Drain the beets and refrigerate until ready to use, up to 2 days.

To cook the grains, bring a large pot of well-salted water to a boil. Add the grains and cook according to the package directions, between 10 minutes for quinoa and over 1 hour for wheat berries. Drain thoroughly, then spread out on a rimmed baking sheet to cool. You should have about 5 cups.

To make the salad, remove the stems from the beet leaves as you would with chard (see Prep Tip, page 85). Thinly slice the stems and cut the leaves into ribbons. Place a large frying pan over medium heat and add 1 teaspoon of the olive oil. Add the garlic and sauté briefly, then add the stems and cook, stirring frequently, until partly tender, about 4 minutes. Add the leaves a few handfuls at a time and cook until wilted, 1 to 2 minutes. Add a splash of water, cover, and cook until the greens and stems are tender, 2 to 3 minutes. Let cool.

Place the cooked grains in a large bowl. Add the beet greens and stems, green onions, herbs, the remaining ¼ cup olive oil, vinegar, ½ teaspoon salt, and ⅛ teaspoon pepper. Toss together and adjust the seasonings. (You can make the salad to this point up to 2 days ahead. Let cool, cover tightly, and refrigerate. Bring to room temperature before serving.)

Place the salad in a serving bowl, top with the drained beets, then the cheese and walnuts. Serve immediately.

BEET GREENS STRATA SERVES 4

Use the beets in the Beet Greens Salad with Whole Grains, Pickled Beets & Fresh Cheese (page 20) or the Scraps Latkes (page 40).

1 teaspoon olive oil, plus more for greasing the pan

Greens from 1 bunch beets, washed (see Prep Tip, page 18)

½ cup finely minced onion, leek, or green onion (white and light green parts)

Kosher salt and freshly ground pepper

1 cup milk

3 large eggs

3 cups bread such as walnut bread, artisan whole wheat, or country bread (preferably day-old or stale), cut into 1-inch cubes

1 cup shredded Gruyère cheese

Like a savory bread pudding, a strata is the perfect brunch dish because you can make it in the evening, perhaps after using the beets in another dish at dinner. You let the bread soak up the custard overnight, and then bake it in the morning. (It's also a fine way to use up extra bread.) On the small side, this recipe uses the greens from one bunch of beets. If you'd like to double it for a larger crowd, just augment with chard or other greens.

Note: If you like, you can add 1 cup cooked and crumbled sausage to the bread when you toss it with the chard.

....

Grease an 8 by 8-inch baking dish with olive oil.

As you would with chard (see Prep Tip, page 85), remove the stems from the beet leaves. Thinly slice the stems and cut the leaves into ribbons. Place a large frying pan over medium heat and add the olive oil. Add the onion and beet stems and cook, stirring frequently, until partly tender, about 4 minutes. Add the leaves a few handfuls at a time and cook until wilted, 1 to 2 minutes. Add a splash of water, cover, and cook until the greens and stems are tender, 2 to 3 minutes. Season with salt and pepper and set aside to cool slightly.

In a medium bowl, combine the milk, eggs, ½ teaspoon salt, and several grindings of pepper. Whisk until smooth.

In a medium bowl, toss the bread with the greens and half of the cheese. Spread the mixture in the prepared

→

pan. Slowly pour the egg mixture over so that the bread is evenly coated. Poke down any pieces of bread that can be further nestled in the custard, then top with the remaining cheese. Cover and refrigerate overnight.

Bring the strata to room temperature for 10 to 20 minutes. Preheat the oven to 350°F.

Bake until the custard is set, the casserole is bubbly, and you can't see any liquid when you press the bread lightly, 40 to 45 minutes. Let cool for 10 minutes before serving.

BRAISED TURNIPS & GREENS WITH SOY BUTTER SERVES 4

Use the dark green part of the leeks in the Crispy Fried Leek Greens (page 65).

1 or 2 bunches young turnips with greens attached or 6 small turnips, washed (see Prep Tip, page 18)

2 tablespoons unsalted butter

1 clove garlic, minced, plus 2 whole cloves garlic, peeled

1 star anise

½ cup very thinly sliced leeks, white part only

Kosher salt

1 cup Vegetable Scraps Stock (page 10) or other vegetable or chicken broth

1 tablespoon soy sauce

1 teaspoon dark brown sugar

Turnip greens are a traditional dish in the South, just like collard greens. In winter and spring, you can often buy bunches of young turnips with their leaves attached; I always try to grab them when I can. These smaller turnips don't need to be peeled like larger ones do, and their leaves are more tender than the larger turnip greens sold separately in bunches. (Mature turnips are usually not sold with their leaves attached.) Here you braise the turnips with leeks and star anise, and then finish the dish with a soy-butter glaze and toss in the wilted greens.

Note: Look for young turnips with their leaves attached in spring at farmers' markets or in Asian markets. If they aren't available, use 1 pound turnips, peeled and cut into ½-inch wedges, and the leaves from a bunch of chard, torn into bite-size pieces. The spice star anise is sold at specialty grocers and Asian markets.

....

Tear the turnip greens into 1 by 2-inch strips and quarter or halve the turnips. If small, the turnips don't need to be peeled.

In a large skillet or wok, melt ½ tablespoon of the butter over medium heat. Add the minced garlic and turnip greens and stir-fry until tender, about 2 minutes. Remove the greens from the wok and set aside.

Add another ½ tablespoon of the butter to the skillet with the star anise, whole garlic cloves, and leeks. Stir-fry for 30 seconds, then add the turnips. Season with salt, stir until coated with butter, and add the stock. Bring to a simmer, partially cover, and cook until the turnips are just tender, 6 to 8 minutes.

Add the remaining 1 tablespoon butter, the soy sauce, and brown sugar. Stir and continue cooking at a simmer until the broth has reduced to a thin glaze, 7 to 8 minutes. During the last 1 to 2 minutes of cooking, return the greens to the pan to heat through. Adjust the seasoning and serve immediately.

RADISH LEAF SALAD WITH CORN, TOMATOES & SALTED CUCUMBERS SERVES 4

Use the cucumber and tomato seeds in the Tomato Water– Cucumber Granita (page 183) and the corn cob in a stock.

Peppery and fresh, radish leaves are tender enough to play the part of lettuce with a spicy kick. Here their spiciness is tempered with sweet corn and tomatoes, as well as cucumbers, which are salted first to firm up their texture. If you like, you can substitute the Avocado-Lemon Dressing with Toasted Cumin (page 170) for the dressing used here.

Note: You don't need to peel English or Persian cucumbers, which have thin skins.

Salad

- 2 Persian cucumbers, or ½ English cucumber
- ½ teaspoon kosher salt
- Leaves from 1 bunch radishes, washed (see Prep Tip, page 18) and dried
- 4 radishes, halved if large, and thinly sliced
- 1 ear of corn, cooked and kernels removed (see Prep Tip, page 144)
- 1 large ripe tomato, seeded and diced
- ¼ cup finely chopped red onions or shallots
- Freshly ground pepper

Dressing

- 3 tablespoons extra-virgin olive oil
- 1½ tablespoons sour cream or plain yogurt
- 1 tablespoon white wine vinegar
- ½ teaspoon honey or sugar
- Kosher salt and freshly ground pepper

To make the salad, quarter or halve the cucumber(s) lengthwise, then scoop out the seeds. Slice the cucumber, place in a small bowl, and toss with ½ teaspoon salt. Let sit for 15 minutes, then rinse, drain, and pat dry.

Meanwhile, remove any stringy stems or yellowed parts from the radish leaves, then tear the leaves into bite-size pieces. Place the radish leaves, radishes, corn, tomato, and onions in a salad bowl.

To make the dressing, whisk together all of the dressing ingredients in a small bowl.

Add the cucumbers to the salad with salt and pepper to taste, toss with the dressing, and serve.

Carrots

Prep Tip

To prepare carrot tops, trim
off the lower thick stems,
then remove any thicker
stems or discolored leaves
in the leafy fronds. Wash and
spin or pat dry.

There are carrots, the nondescript chunky numbers we
chop for soup and chicken stock, and then there are carrots, the tender babes that are so sweet and carroty they
bring up memories of childhood tastes from a backyard
vegetable patch. Old botanical prints show carrots of the
purest white, yellow, and purple and in all kinds of shapes.
Look for these unusually colored heirloom carrots, such
as the cute and stubby Chantenay and the more cylindrical and elegant Nantes, in specialty stores and farmers'
markets. True baby carrots are so beautiful and tender
that you don't even need to peel them lest you remove too
much of their flesh and flavor. Just scrub and trim them.

Buying carrots with the bright greens attached—an
unmistakable indicator of freshness—is a worthwhile
splurge for carrot-centric recipes. Plus, the greens do a
fine job of standing in for parsley when finely chopped,
leaving you one less herb to buy. That's especially true in
the Italian herb sauce salsa verde (page 34), where their
slightly bitter flavor is balanced with salty anchovies and
capers as well as fresh thyme, oregano, and rosemary. The
greens also make a light version of tabbouleh (page 36) and
are refreshing combined with grated carrots in a slaw with
a yogurt-coriander dressing (page 31). If you can't find
carrots with the tops attached and still would like to make
one of these recipes, use Italian parsley instead.

To store, remove the tops from the carrots and wrap
them, unwashed, in a plastic bag in the refrigerator. Greens
and tops will keep for 2 days and carrots will keep for
several weeks.

CARROT SLAW WITH GREEK YOGURT, LEMON & CORIANDER SERVES 4 TO 6

Use up any extra carrot greens in the Carrot Top Salsa Verde (page 34).

¼ cup plain Greek or other thick yogurt

3 tablespoons fresh lemon juice, preferably Meyer lemon

2 tablespoons extra-virgin olive oil

2 teaspoons honey

½ teaspoon ground cumin

½ teaspoon ground coriander

Kosher salt and freshly ground pepper

5 cups coarsely grated carrots (from 1 or 2 bunches)

⅓ cup finely chopped carrot tops

¼ cup sultanas (golden raisins)

¼ cup toasted slivered almonds

This recipe is based on a favorite salad my mom used to make when I was growing up, which had a creamy dressing, cinnamon, and raisins. I remember helping her grate the carrots with a mint-green Tupperware grater that attached to a matching bowl. In this version, Greek yogurt and lemon help incorporate the slight bitterness of the carrot tops into the mix of sweet carrots, raisins, and warm spices like coriander, which has citrusy notes that heighten carrots' natural sweetness.

Note: A bunch of carrots can range a lot in size; you'll need about 6 medium carrots.

Combine the yogurt, lemon juice, olive oil, honey, cumin, coriander, and salt and pepper to taste in a salad bowl and whisk to combine.

Add the carrots, carrot tops, and sultanas. Toss and add more salt and pepper to taste if needed. Serve immediately or refrigerate for several hours before serving. Sprinkle with the almonds to serve.

Carrot Top Salsa Verde with Roasted Root Vegetables

CARROT TOP SALSA VERDE WITH ROASTED ROOT VEGETABLES SERVES 6

Salsa verde

- 5 anchovy fillets
- 3 tablespoons capers (soaked in water if salted), drained
- 2 whole cloves garlic, peeled
- Tops from 1 bunch carrots (about 3 cups coarsely chopped), washed well (see Prep Tip, page 30) and chopped
- 1 tablespoon fresh rosemary
- 1 tablespoon fresh oregano or other tender herbs, such as chives, fennel fronds, or marjoram
- 2 teaspoons fresh thyme
- ¼ teaspoon red chile flakes
- 1 tablespoon fresh lemon juice, plus more to taste
- ⅔ cup extra-virgin olive oil
- Freshly ground pepper

Not to be confused with Mexican salsa verde, Italian salsa verde is a fresh sauce traditionally made with parsley, anchovies, capers, lemon, and flavorful herbs. Here you use carrot tops instead of parsley, and the carrots themselves help sweeten up the accompanying mixture of starchy roasted root vegetables, a classic wintertime side dish. You'll probably have leftover sauce, which is fantastic with the Fennel-Roasted Whole Fish with Potatoes (page 58).

Note: You can substitute 3 cups chopped Italian parsley, thick lower stems removed, for the carrot tops or add some fennel fronds.

To make the salsa verde, place the anchovies, capers, and garlic in a food processor and pulse until finely chopped. Add the carrot tops, rosemary, oregano, thyme, red chile flakes, and lemon juice and process until finely chopped. With the processor running, gradually pour in the olive oil through the feed tube and puree until very smooth. Season to taste with pepper and more lemon juice, if you like. (The sauce can be stored in the refrigerator, tightly covered, for 2 days before serving.)

Roasted vegetables

- 1 pound fingerling or small Yukon gold potatoes, halved
- 1 bunch carrots, peeled or scrubbed and halved lengthwise
- 1 pound parsnips or turnips, cut into long wedges
- 2 tablespoons olive oil

  Kosher salt and freshly ground pepper

To make the roasted vegetables, preheat the oven to 400°F.

Place the potatoes, carrots, and parsnips in a large bowl with the olive oil and salt and pepper to taste. Toss to coat, then spread the vegetables out in a single layer on two rimmed baking sheets with the potatoes cut side down. Roast until the vegetables are tender and golden, 30 to 40 minutes, flipping the potatoes and stirring the other vegetables halfway through and removing vegetables as they are done.

Serve the vegetables warm, drizzled with some of the salsa verde.

QUINOA-CARROT TABBOULEH SERVES 6

1 cup quinoa

2 cups water

¾ teaspoon kosher salt

Tops from 1 bunch carrots (about 3 cups chopped), washed (see Prep Tip, page 30) and finely chopped

2 small carrots, peeled or scrubbed and shaved with a peeler into thin coins

1 cup diced English cucumber

2 small tomatoes, chopped

½ cup finely chopped green onions, white and green parts

¼ cup finely chopped fresh mint

Juice of 1 to 2 lemons

¼ cup olive oil

Freshly ground pepper

Although tabbouleh traditionally contains bulgur wheat and other vegetables, it's really all about the parsley, which is used in generous quantities. Here, however, carrot tops take the place of the herb, and quinoa replaces traditional bulgur to mix things up. Adding fresh carrots in the form of paper-thin rounds made with a vegetable peeler provides sweetness and color.

Note: You can substitute 3 cups chopped Italian parsley, thick lower stems removed, for the carrot tops.

....

Rinse the quinoa in a fine-mesh strainer and drain. Place the quinoa with the water and ¼ teaspoon of the salt in a small saucepan and bring to a simmer. Cover and cook until the water is absorbed and the grains are tender, 10 to 12 minutes. Spread the quinoa out on a rimmed baking sheet to cool.

Place the quinoa in a large bowl with the carrot tops, carrots, cucumber, tomatoes, green onions, mint, the juice of 1 lemon, and the remaining ½ teaspoon salt. Toss and let sit for 10 minutes as the quinoa absorbs the liquid and the flavors combine, then add the olive oil and pepper to taste. Add more lemon and salt to taste, then serve at room temperature.

Potatoes

Potatoes are usually associated with abundance, except for the famine that brought my Irish ancestors to this country in the nineteenth century. Cooking with them means being left with piles of potato peels and the inevitable trimmings that happen when you try to chop a round object into something with right angles, such as cubes for a chowder or batons for French fries. Whenever I mash, boil, or roast potatoes, I always make too many, maybe because of a deep-rooted ancestral fear.

Potato skins contain a lot of nutrients, including fiber, vitamins, and iron, and, as we may remember from happy hour menus, they are delicious when fried. Toss them with bacon fat and a spice mixture and roast them in the oven and the soggy peels turn into smoky, crispy chips (page 38). And if you find yourself with lots of extra potato trimmings—or scraps from other starchy raw vegetables—there's a wildcard recipe for Scraps Latkes (page 40), a version of potato pancakes made from all kinds of shredded root vegetables.

When storing potatoes, keep them in a cool place away from light; don't hold them in the refrigerator unless they are true new potatoes, which have not been cured for room-temperature storage.

Prep Tip

If you peel or chop potatoes ahead of time, place the peels or potato scraps in a bowl of water to prevent them from browning. When you're ready to cook them, drain, then wring them dry in a clean kitchen towel.

POTATO SKIN-BACON FAT CHIPS SERVES 4

Making use of potato skins and rendered bacon fat, this crispy snack can be a byproduct of making Smoky Corn Cob Chowder (page 145), which calls for both peeled potatoes and bacon. That recipe uses only enough potatoes to make a half a batch of these chips, but it's still plenty for a small appetizer. The slight bitterness of the potato skins is matched by an assertive brown sugar spice mix and the smokiness from the bacon. You can tell these chips are done when the bacon aroma becomes unmistakable.

1 teaspoon dark brown sugar

½ teaspoon kosher salt

¼ teaspoon sweet paprika

¼ teaspoon freshly ground pepper

1 teaspoon chopped fresh thyme, or ½ teaspoon dried

Skin peelings from 4 russet potatoes

2 tablespoons bacon fat, warmed until liquid, or olive oil

Preheat the oven to 400°F.

In a small bowl, combine the brown sugar, salt, paprika, pepper, and thyme.

Place the potato skins in a medium bowl and pour the bacon fat over, then sprinkle with half of the spice mixture. Turn the potatoes to coat evenly in the fat and spices.

Spread the skins on a baking sheet evenly, making sure that most of the pieces are in contact with the bottom of the pan (this helps ensure they turn crispy). Sprinkle with the remaining spice mixture and bake until the potato skins are starting to become crispy and golden, 12 minutes. Stir and continue cooking until uniformly crispy, 3 to 6 minutes more. Serve right away on a plate lined with paper towels.

SCRAPS LATKES MAKES 20 SMALL LATKES; SERVES 4 TO 6

Traditionally fried up during Hanukkah, latkes are simply pancakes made of shredded potatoes bound with eggs. This version uses any kind of scraps you may have, such as odds and ends that remain after cutting up and trimming vegetables for a soup. Just throw the vegetable ends in the food processor with the grating attachment to shred them. These crispy mini-latkes make a delicious appetizer with sour cream and applesauce any time of the year.

Note: If you don't have scraps, just use one whole carrot, one beet, and one russet potato.

3 cups peeled and grated raw root vegetables or tubers, such as potatoes, sweet potatoes, beets, carrots, parsnips, turnips, or celery root

¼ onion, very thinly sliced or shredded in a food processor

2 large eggs

1 tablespoon cornstarch

½ teaspoon baking powder

½ teaspoon kosher salt

¼ teaspoon freshly ground pepper

Olive oil or vegetable oil

Sour cream and applesauce, to serve

Preheat the oven to 200°F. Line a baking sheet with paper towels.

Place the grated vegetables and onion in a large bowl. Add the eggs, cornstarch, baking powder, salt, and pepper and stir well.

Place a large frying pan over medium-low to medium heat and add enough oil to fill the pan to a depth of ¼ to ½ inch. When the oil is hot, use a soup spoon to scoop up about 2 tablespoonfuls of the latke mixture, then use another soup spoon to press down on the mixture to make an oval patty. Gently slide the patty into the oil. Continue making patties with the spoons and cook 6 to 8 latkes at a time, without crowding them, until browned, crisp, and cooked through, about 5 minutes per side. Make sure the oil isn't too hot or they will burn.

Place the latkes on the prepared baking sheet and keep warm in the oven while you finish the rest. Season with salt and serve with the sour cream and applesauce.

BULBS & STEMS

Eating stems brings to mind chewing on sour grass as a kid, sucking out the puckery juices while chomping down on the thin, crunchy stems topped with yellow flowers. Yet we actually eat stems all the time in the form of one of the most common vegetables: celery. Asparagus is another type of edible stem, which I've paired up with bulbs in this chapter, a botanical class that includes onions, garlic, leeks, and fennel. I focus on leeks and fennel especially because, unlike garlic and onions, they are perishable, and both have so many parts that get wasted. Fennel's long stalks can stand in for celery with extra sweetness and an anise-like flavor, and its feathery fronds are beautiful in salads and sauces. Meanwhile, leek greens, the dark part of the leek that most recipes tell you to throw out, are actually a delicious vegetable in their own right.

Season: Asparagus is a springtime vegetable, leeks' prime time is spring and fall, and fennel and celery are available year round.

Asparagus Stalk Stock **47**

Asparagus, Artichoke & Chickpea Ragout **49**

Creamy Asparagus & Celery Heart Soup with Tarragon **50**

Celery Slaw with Apple Peel & Ginger Dressing **52**

Steamed Mussels with Celery Leaf Salad **53**

Fennel Parmesan Salad **55**

Fennel-Roasted Whole Fish with Potatoes **58**

Fennel-Braised Pork Roast **61**

Candied Fennel Stalk & Fennel Syrup **63**

Crispy Fried Leek Greens **65**

Leek Greens Stir-Fry with Salty Pork Belly **67**

Leek Greens & Shrimp Pot Stickers **68**

Beans & Leek Greens Soup **72**

Asparagus

Prep Tip

To trim asparagus stalks, bend the bottom end of each stalk until the tough part snaps off.

If you've ever seen asparagus in the field you'll agree it's a truly weird vegetable. An older patch resembles a field of long fernlike grasses until you look closer and realize there are tender stalks of asparagus, with their characteristic flowery tips, peeking up through the grass. At larger farms, the stalks just shoot right up through the dark soil, like something from an alien planet.

Michigan, Washington, and California are all big asparagus-growing states, and the asparagus grown in the Sacramento–San Joaquin River delta, near where I live, has a cultlike following. Like all cultish things, the fat stalks are available for only a short period of time. Even harder to find is wild asparagus, a smaller vinelike variety with teeny-tiny tips that occasionally shows up in restaurants.

Each stalk of asparagus has to be harvested by hand, one reason why it's expensive. The edible part of an asparagus plant is its young shoots; once the feathery tops flower, the stalks will turn tough. (That's one reason to always select asparagus with tight, fresh-looking tips.) Once asparagus is harvested, the cut ends start to toughen up; that's why you have to discard the bottoms, which can account for about one-third the weight of the stalks. But you can easily make use of this waste by making the Asparagus Stalk Stock (page 47), which goes into both Creamy Asparagus & Celery Heart Soup with Tarragon (page 50) and the springtime Asparagus, Artichoke & Chickpea Ragout (page 49).

To store asparagus, keep it in a plastic bag in the refrigerator for up to 2 days.

ASPARAGUS STALK STOCK MAKES 6 TO 7 CUPS

5 or 6 cups asparagus stalk ends, from about five 1-pound bunches of asparagus

10 cups water

1 cup coarsely chopped celery or celery hearts

1 cup coarsely chopped onion or leeks, white and green parts

5 peppercorns

1 bay leaf

1 sprig thyme

While you can make stock out of just about any vegetable scraps—with the exception of artichoke leaves, which result in a bitter, stinky brew—asparagus trimmings are one of the best items to save up for making stock, especially since the vegetable can be a luxury ingredient. Since the stalks from one bunch of asparagus aren't enough to make stock—you'll need the trimmings from about five bunches—just put your trimmed stalks in a zip-top bag in the freezer each time you prepare asparagus. The result is an intensively flavored stock that makes soups and vegetarian dishes especially bright and springlike.

Place all of the ingredients in a medium stockpot. Bring to a simmer, then simmer gently for 30 minutes. Strain, discarding the solids. Let the stock cool completely, then cover tightly. The stock can be refrigerated for 5 days or frozen for 2 months.

ASPARAGUS, ARTICHOKE & CHICKPEA RAGOUT SERVES 4

Use the asparagus stems in the Asparagus Stalk Stock (page 47) and the leftover artichoke leaves in the Roasted Artichoke Leaves (page 123).

¼ cup extra-virgin olive oil

2 artichokes, trimmed to the heart and tender inner leaves (see Prep Tip, page 122), and sliced into ½-inch wedges

1 cup sliced spring onion

¼ teaspoon red chile flakes

2 cloves garlic, thinly sliced

2 cups Asparagus Stalk Stock (page 47) or other vegetable or chicken broth

½ teaspoon kosher salt

1 bunch asparagus (1 pound), trimmed and cut into 1½-inch lengths

1½ to 2 cups cooked chickpeas, or 1 (14-ounce) can chickpeas, drained and rinsed

1 to 2 tablespoons fresh lemon juice

1 tablespoon thinly sliced fresh mint

1 teaspoon finely chopped fresh thyme

Freshly ground pepper

My three favorite vegetables form a trinity of *A* words: asparagus, artichokes, and avocado. (Okay, avocado is really a fruit; see page 159.) As a native Californian, I was raised on these three foods, and this recipe happily includes two of them. With their heady flavor and meaty texture, seared artichoke hearts make an intriguing contrast with sweet, tender pieces of asparagus. This vegetarian stew combines them with chickpeas in a light broth flavored with a springtime combination of mint, thyme, and lemon. Serve the ragout in bowls with bread on the side, or over penne pasta with shaved Parmesan.

Note: When trimming the artichoke hearts, be sure to remove all dark green parts, which are tough and inedible.

....

In a large skillet, heat the olive oil over medium heat. Add the artichoke hearts, onion, and red chile flakes and sauté until browned, 4 to 5 minutes. Add the garlic and cook, stirring, until fragrant, about 1 minute. Add 1 cup of the asparagus stock and the salt. Bring to a simmer, cover, and cook until the artichoke hearts are tender when pierced with a knife, 4 to 5 minutes. Add the asparagus and cook, stirring, over medium heat until just tender, 2 to 3 minutes.

Add the remaining 1 cup stock with the chickpeas, 1 tablespoon of the lemon juice, mint, and thyme. Simmer until the flavors come together, about 3 minutes. Season to taste with salt and pepper and more lemon juice, and serve.

CREAMY ASPARAGUS & CELERY HEART SOUP WITH TARRAGON SERVES 4

Use the asparagus stems in the Asparagus Stalk Stock (page 47) and the potato peels for the Potato Skin–Bacon Fat Chips (page 38).

1 bunch asparagus (1 pound), trimmed (see Prep Tip, page 46)

2 tablespoons extra-virgin olive oil

½ cup chopped celery hearts and leaves

1 spring onion, or 3 green onions, including half of the dark green parts, sliced, white and green parts kept separate

1 small russet potato, peeled and cut into ½-inch cubes

3 cups Asparagus Stalk Stock (page 47) or other vegetable or chicken broth

Kosher and freshly ground pepper

¼ cup heavy cream

2 teaspoons chopped fresh tarragon

Drizzle of champagne vinegar or fresh lemon juice

This soup is silky smooth because the asparagus cooks with the potatoes until it is totally soft, so there are no tough fibers left when you puree it. Preparing this with the Asparagus Stalk Stock can make the difference between a simple soup and one that is striking in its asparagus flavor—not bad considering it only uses one bunch of asparagus. A splash of cream adds an extra bit of richness at the end.

. . . .

Reserve the asparagus tips (the top 2 inches or so) from the asparagus and slice them in half lengthwise, then slice the stalks into ½-inch pieces.

Place the olive oil in a medium saucepan over medium heat. When the oil is shimmering, add the asparagus tips and sauté until browned and tender, about 3 minutes. Remove with a slotted spoon and set aside for a garnish.

Add the celery and the whites of the onion and sauté until lightly browned, 4 minutes. Add the asparagus stalks, potato, and stock and bring to a simmer. Cover and cook until the potato is completely tender, 18 to 20 minutes. During the last 5 minutes of cooking, add the onion greens.

Remove from the heat and puree the soup in a blender or with an immersion blender until very smooth, then season with salt and pepper to taste. Add the cream, tarragon, and vinegar, then puree again and taste to see if it needs more salt, pepper, or vinegar. Serve immediately in shallow bowls garnished with the asparagus tips.

Celery

The main type of celery we eat is cultivated for its dark green outer stalks and pale inner stalks, which are essentially exaggerated stems. Other celery varieties are grown for the bulbous root—celeriac—or the leafy green tops. The latter is known as soup celery or Chinese celery, an intense variety that appeals to folks who love bitter vegetables with a mineral-like flavor. All display varying degrees of stalk celery's pleasant, refreshing flavor, which adds balance to sweeter onions and carrots in the base of a soup, or can be assertive and interesting on its own.

Celery shows up in various guises throughout this book, often as a central player, to avoid it going bad before you use it all. Rather than waste it, embrace it: for example, use it thinly sliced for slaws or salads, such as the Celery Slaw with Apple Peel & Ginger Dressing (page 52). Or use celery as a substitute for fennel in the Fennel Parmesan Salad (page 55).

The tender leaves and inner stalks from a large bunch of celery tend to get ignored or discarded, yet they actually have a more concentrated flavor and delicate texture than the large outer stalks. Use them to add another dimension to a creamy asparagus soup (page 50), or use the leaves and hearts in a refreshing garnish for steamed mussels (page 53).

Store celery wrapped in damp paper towels in a plastic bag in the refrigerator for 1 to 2 weeks.

CELERY SLAW WITH APPLE PEEL & GINGER DRESSING SERVES 4 TO 6

Use any remaining cabbage in the Sauerkraut (page 83). You can also add peeled and julienned broccoli stalk (see Prep Tip, page 127) to this recipe as a replacement for part of the cabbage or celery.

Usually thought of as a summer dish, slaw turns into a vibrant fall salad with the addition of apples, ginger, and, in this case, celery. This salad calls for about half of an average-sized cabbage, so it's a good way to use up any leftovers in your refrigerator. Although julienned apple peels make a pretty, not to mention thrifty, accent to this salad, use them only if you are peeling apples for another dish, such as a dessert or apple butter. Otherwise just use julienned strips of whole apple, preferably a tart variety like Granny Smith.

Note: To julienne apple peels, trim any long peels into 2-inch lengths. Stack a few peels and thinly slice, then repeat with any remaining peels. If you don't have fresh ginger on hand, substitute 1 to 2 teaspoons of whole-grain or Dijon mustard.

Dressing

- 3 tablespoons apple cider vinegar
- 2 teaspoons finely grated fresh ginger
- 1½ teaspoons honey
- ½ teaspoon kosher salt
- Freshly ground pepper
- Pinch of finely chopped fresh thyme
- ¼ cup plus 1 tablespoon vegetable oil

- 1 pound napa, red, or green cabbage, cored and shredded (7 to 8 cups)
- 3 inner or outer stalks celery, very thinly sliced on the diagonal
- Julienned peels of 2 apples (see Note), or 1 whole apple, cored and julienned
- Kosher salt and freshly ground pepper

To make the dressing, whisk together the vinegar, ginger, honey, salt, pepper to taste, and thyme in a small bowl. Slowly whisk in the vegetable oil until emulsified.

Place the cabbage, celery, and apple in a large salad bowl. Toss with the dressing and plenty of salt and pepper to taste.

The slaw can be made and refrigerated 2 hours ahead if using napa cabbage, which will wilt if kept any longer, but it can be made 4 hours ahead if using red or green cabbage, which improves with time.

STEAMED MUSSELS WITH CELERY LEAF SALAD SERVES 4

Use extra celery in the Fennel-Braised Pork Roast (page 61).

Salad

2 cups tender leaves and thinly sliced inner hearts from 1 bunch celery

2 jarred piquillo peppers or roasted and peeled red bell peppers, cut into thin strips

2 tablespoons extra-virgin olive oil

1 tablespoon fresh lemon juice

Kosher salt and freshly ground pepper

Mussels

2 tablespoons olive oil

3 outer stalks celery, sliced ½ inch thick

½ onion, sliced, or 1 cup sliced leeks, white part only

4 whole cloves garlic, peeled and lightly crushed

4 thin strips lemon zest

1 small dried red chile, torn in half

1 bay leaf

1 cup dry white wine

3 pounds mussels, scrubbed and debearded if needed

Kosher salt and freshly ground pepper

With its mild astringency and juicy freshness, celery is a wonderful foil to strongly flavored seafood. In this recipe you use the outer celery stalks to steam mussels and then serve them with a cold celery leaf salad for crunch and flavor. The salad is also delicious served as an appetizer with marinated sardines purchased at an Italian deli, or with any fried seafood (think shrimp po' boy). Don't forget to pick up a baguette for dipping into the juices.

To make the salad, place the celery leaves and hearts and piquillo peppers in a large bowl and toss with the olive oil, lemon juice, and salt and pepper to taste. Set aside or refrigerate for up to 2 hours.

To make the mussels, heat the olive oil in a large stockpot or Dutch oven over medium heat. Add the celery, onion, garlic, lemon zest, chile, and bay leaf and cook until the vegetables are tender, 8 minutes. Add the wine and simmer for 1 to 2 minutes. Add the mussels, season with salt and pepper, and bring to a simmer. Reduce the heat to medium-low and steam the mussels, covered, until they are plump and their shells have opened wide, 4 to 5 minutes. Discard any mussels that did not open.

Serve the hot mussels out of the pot, either with the salad on the side or as a garnish on top of the mussels.

Fennel

Italians love fennel so much that they brought it over to California when they first immigrated here in the nineteenth century. It turned out to be an invasive species that now grows wild all over the state. Our apartment is perched above a gully leading down to a busy road, an open city-owned space that is completely covered in wild fennel. Work crews cut it back from time to time, but it always returns, growing eight feet high in summer, when it is crowned with dusty yellow blossoms. Its licorice scent is everywhere.

Luckily we love fennel—how it bridges the gap between sweet and savory flavors—and we sometimes reach over our back fence to harvest the fennel greens or pollen to flavor fish and meat, as well as drinks and desserts. Our girls and their friends collect the greens and toss it with sugar to make what they called fennel candy, then they sell the sticky fronds at their lemonade stand.

Wild fennel is a different variety than bulb fennel, also called Florence fennel, the kind we love to eat in salads. Because bulb fennel can be expensive and so much of it goes to waste, I've always tried to find uses for its long, tough stalks, which have a stronger anise flavor than the bulbs, and its tender fronds. Sadly, much of the fennel sold in stores has its fronds chopped off, but the fennel you find in farmers' markets is usually abundant with greens and stalks.

To store fennel, keep it in a plastic bag in the refrigerator for up to a week.

Prep Tip

Like cabbage, fennel bulbs have a hard core in the center. To core a fennel bulb, quarter it lengthwise, then remove the core in the center of each piece with a diagonal cut.

FENNEL PARMESAN SALAD SERVES 4

2 fennel stalks, very thinly sliced on the diagonal, plus 1 small fennel bulb, cored (see Prep Tip, page 54) and thinly sliced

Chunk of Parmigiano-Reggiano cheese

2 tablespoons extra-virgin olive oil

1 tablespoon fresh lemon juice

Kosher salt and freshly ground pepper

Chopped fennel fronds

I learned how to make this salad from a friend during the semester that I dropped out of college to waitress at a Mexican restaurant in Milan, Italy (my parents were thrilled). I was amazed by the sweetness of the juicy white vegetable against the smooth, buttery olive oil, shards of salty Parmesan, and sharp lemon juice and pepper. It's a magic combination that I returned to often after coming home (and eventually graduating from college). I still make it often when we don't have any lettuce but do have part of a fennel bulb or fennel stalks left over from another recipe.

Note: Celery stalks, thinly sliced on the diagonal, and thinly sliced trimmed broccoli stems (see Prep Tip, page 127) are also delicious in this salad, either alone or combined with the fennel.

Place the sliced fennel stalks and bulb in a medium bowl. Using a sharp vegetable peeler, shave the Parmesan in thin shards over the fennel.

Add the olive oil, lemon juice, and salt and pepper to taste. Toss the salad gently, then adjust the seasoning with more salt and pepper if necessary. Shave more Parmesan on top, sprinkle with the fennel fronds, and serve immediately.

Fennel-Roasted Whole Fish with Potatoes

FENNEL-ROASTED WHOLE FISH WITH POTATOES SERVES 4

2 large fennel bulbs, with stalks and fronds attached

3 to 4 tablespoons olive oil, plus more for drizzling

1 lemon, halved

Kosher salt and freshly ground pepper

1½ pounds small new potatoes

2 small branzini or other whole fish, 1 pound each, gutted and scaled

Carrot Top Salsa Verde (page 34; optional)

Just like cooking with whole vegetables, whole fish cookery is easy to master. Not only is roasting a whole fish dramatic, but it results in juicy fillets and lots of extra flavor. In this recipe, stuffing fennel fronds into the fish's cavity during roasting adds even more intensity. Channel your inner old-fashioned waiter by serving the fillets from the whole fish at the table. The fish is delicious as is but even better with a piquant herb sauce, such as Carrot Top Salsa Verde (page 34). You can even add some of the extra fennel fronds to the sauce.

Note: Look for branzini or other whole fish at seafood markets and well-stocked supermarkets. Another option is whole trout, which only takes 20 to 25 minutes to roast.

Preheat the oven to 400°F and arrange racks in the upper and lower thirds of the oven.

Remove the stalks and fronds from the fennel and separate the two. Thinly slice enough of the stalks to get ½ to 1 cup. Set aside.

Core the fennel bulb (see Prep Tip, page 54), then slice ½ inch thick. In a medium bowl, toss the fennel slices with 2 tablespoons of the olive oil and the juice of a half lemon, plus salt and pepper to taste. Place in a 9 by 13-inch baking dish or gratin dish large enough to fit both fish.

Toss the potatoes in enough olive oil to coat thoroughly, 1 to 2 tablespoons, and season to taste with salt. Spread out on a baking sheet. Place the fennel and potatoes on separate racks in the oven and roast until the fennel is

Prep Tip

To fillet a cooked whole fish, at the tail, make a shallow cut through the top fillet down to the backbone. Holding the tail in one hand, run a flat knife from the cut in the tail along the backbone until you reach the gills. Lift the fillet off the backbone onto a serving plate. Remove the head and backbone, leaving the bottom fillet boneless. Flip that fillet, remove to another serving plate, and repeat with the other fish. (Watch for small stray bones in the fillets.)

starting to become tender, 30 minutes, stirring both halfway through roasting.

Meanwhile, make three slits on both sides of each fish fillet and season the fish well on all sides, inside and out, with salt and pepper. Stuff the cavities with all of the fronds and as much of the sliced stalks you can fit. Thinly slice the remaining lemon half and stuff the slices inside the fish.

Top the roasted fennel with the prepared fish and drizzle the fish with olive oil. Roast until the whole fish, including the bottom fillets, is thoroughly cooked (the slits will be opaque), 35 to 40 minutes. Meanwhile, continue cooking the potatoes until golden and tender when pierced with a knife, another 10 to 30 minutes.

Discard the fronds and stalks inside the fish, then remove the fish fillets from the bone (see Prep Tip, opposite). Serve the fillets immediately with the roasted fennel bulb and potatoes, and the Carrot Top Salsa Verde on the side, if you like.

FENNEL-BRAISED PORK ROAST SERVES 8

Use the celery hearts in the Creamy Asparagus & Celery Heart Soup with Tarragon (page 50) or the Celery Slaw with Apple Peel & Ginger Dressing (page 52).

4 pounds bone-in, or 3 to 3½ pounds boneless, pork butt or other shoulder roast, rolled and tied

Kosher salt and freshly ground pepper

2 large fennel bulbs, with stalks and fronds

2 large leeks, washed (see Prep Tip, page 64) and trimmed

Vegetable or olive oil

3 stalks celery, sliced into 3-inch pieces

1 cup dry white wine

2 sprigs thyme

2 sprigs rosemary

2 bay leaves

½ teaspoon fennel seeds (optional)

3 cups low-sodium chicken or pork broth

Fennel and pork are paired often in Italian cooking, such as with the fennel seeds in Italian pork sausage. Pork benefits from sweeter ingredients, and fennel's licorice flavor seems to be the right balance for the rich meat. In this preparation, you braise pork roast with fennel stalks and leek greens, and later add to the pot the white part of the leeks and the fennel bulbs, which are left in large pieces so they don't overcook and can be served with the meat.

Note: Bone-in pork roast is harder to find than boneless but is more flavorful. Ask your butcher to roll and tie the roast for you. As with all braises, this is best served the next day, when it is also easier to remove the fat. Let the meat rest in the liquid and refrigerate overnight, then skim off the hardened fat on top.

Preheat the oven to 325°F.

Season the pork roast liberally with salt and pepper on all sides and leave at room temperature while you prepare the vegetables.

Remove the stalks and fronds from the fennel (reserve and chop some of the fronds to garnish the roast) and chop the stalks into 2-inch chunks. Quarter the bulbs, leaving in the core so they stay intact. Then thickly slice the dark green parts of the leeks to get 1½ cups and cut the white parts into 3-inch lengths. Set aside the fennel bulbs and leek whites.

Heat enough oil to liberally cover the bottom of a Dutch oven over medium to medium-high heat. When the oil is hot, brown the roast until golden all over, 3 to 5 minutes per side. Remove from the pan and pour off all but 1 to 2 tablespoons of fat. Add the leek greens, fennel stalks and fronds, and celery to the pan and cook, stirring to coat, for 2 minutes. Add the wine, deglaze the pan, and simmer for 1 to 2 minutes.

Nestle the pork into the vegetables fat side up. Add the thyme, rosemary, bay leaves, and fennel seeds. Pour enough broth to reach halfway up the side of the roast (if you need more liquid, add water), then bring it to a simmer.

Cover, place in the oven, and roast for 30 minutes, then remove from the oven. The broth should be at a low simmer; if not, adjust the oven temperature. Flip the roast and continue cooking and flipping every 30 minutes until the meat is fork tender, about 3 hours total. After 2 hours, add the leek whites and fennel bulbs.

Remove the pork roast and leek whites and fennel bulb pieces from the Dutch oven, then strain the juices and use a large spoon to scoop off as much of the fat floating on the top as you can. Wipe out the pot, return the juices to the pan, and simmer until thickened, about 10 minutes.

To serve, return the meat, fennel bulbs, and leek whites to the Dutch oven and gently rewarm on the stove. Remove the strings from the roast, slice the meat into pieces 1 inch thick, and serve with the juices and vegetables, garnished with the reserved fennel fronds.

CANDIED FENNEL STALK & FENNEL SYRUP
MAKES ¾ CUP CANDY AND 1 CUP SYRUP

1 cup sugar

1 cup water

1½ cups fennel stalks, thinly sliced on the diagonal

Similar to the technique for preserving citrus peel, this recipe uses up the fennel stalks that often go to waste, turning them into a chewy anise-flavored candy. Because fennel stalks are fibrous, make sure to slice them thinly and to let them dry out completely in the oven; the candy will crisp as it cools. Eat the candied fennel out of hand, or use it to garnish fruit salads, desserts, or cocktails.

You will also be left with a fennel-flavored syrup that works as a substitute for simple syrup in fresh lemonade or harder drinks. The subtle fennel flavor is somewhat lost next to strongly flavored spirits, so it helps to add fennel fronds to the drink, muddled with the syrup. For more on infused syrups, see page 189.

Preheat the oven to 250°F.

Place the sugar and water in a small saucepan and cook over medium heat, until the sugar is dissolved, about 5 minutes. Add the fennel, bring to a simmer, and cook until crisp-tender (it will still be fibrous), about 3 minutes. Let the fennel sit in the syrup for 10 to 15 minutes, then strain, reserving the syrup.

Spread the fennel out on a baking sheet lined with parchment paper or a Silpat mat and bake in the oven until dry and sticky, about 1 hour. After 30 minutes of baking, separate any clumps (this is easier to do when they're partly dry) so that all of the slices are in a single layer.

Let the fennel cool completely on the pan, then serve. The candy will keep for up to 4 days at room temperature, and the syrup will keep for 2 weeks in the refrigerator, stored in an airtight container.

Leeks

Leeks have a few things going against them. They are more expensive than onions, and more cumbersome since they are so big and need to be refrigerated. Plus, they need to be thoroughly washed since they're always muddy in between their layers of leaves. Yet I love their mild flavor and tender texture and how they take very little time to soften in the pan. You can add huge piles of them to soups and baked dishes for extra volume, silkiness, and a subtle onion flavor that suits mild ingredients like potatoes, cream, eggs, and fresh cheeses.

After all the trouble you go to for leeks, it seems a terrible waste to use only the white and light green parts and to throw out the dark green parts, as most recipes call for. I assumed that leek greens were inedible until I discovered that they can be cooked like braising greens, with the added benefit of a chive-like flavor. However, because they are more fibrous than the white parts, they need to be cooked a little longer. Now I use leek greens as much as I can, in stir-fries (page 67), in soups like Beans & Leek Greens Soup (page 72), and even as a stuffing for shrimp pot stickers (page 68). In addition to the recipes that follow, the Fennel-Braised Pork Roast (page 61) and the Romaine Leaf Soup with Leeks and Peas (page 114) also make use of leek greens.

Leeks can be stored in a plastic bag in the refrigerator for 1 week.

Prep Tip

To wash leeks, trim off the roots while leaving the very bottom intact so that the layers stay together. Cut the leek in half down its length. Wash under running water, rinsing out as much of the dirt between the layers, especially the dark green parts, as you can. Chop or slice as directed, then place the pieces in a bowl of water and soak to remove any remaining dirt. Use a slotted spoon or skimmer to lift the slices out, leaving the grit behind.

CRISPY FRIED LEEK GREENS MAKES ½ CUP

1 cup vegetable oil

½ cup very thinly sliced leek greens, washed (see Prep Tip, page 64) and well dried

Kosher salt to taste

In restaurants, cooks often use fried leek greens to give dishes visual appeal and add a charred oniony flavor. Because leek greens are tough, however, it's difficult to cook them until they are crispy rather than chewy. The trick is to use plenty of oil that's hot but not so hot that the greens burn. When done, they should be quite brown, almost—but not quite—black.

Use the fried greens to garnish fish dishes or soups such as the Beans & Leek Greens Soup (page 72).

Note: To prevent excessive spattering, it's important to dry leek greens thoroughly before frying them. If you have time, wash and slice the leeks in advance and leave them out to dry on a baking sheet lined with a kitchen towel overnight or for a few hours before frying.

Place the vegetable oil in a small, deep saucepan over medium heat. When it reaches 350°F on a deep-fry thermometer, add the greens. Cook until browned and crispy, 1 to 1½ minutes. Remove with a skimmer or slotted spoon to a paper towel–lined plate.

Season with salt and serve immediately, or allow to cool completely, then store in a paper towel–lined airtight container at room temperature for up to 2 days.

LEEK GREENS STIR-FRY
WITH SALTY PORK BELLY SERVES 4

1 tablespoon vegetable oil

4 whole cloves garlic, peeled and crushed with the side of a knife

10 to 15 Chinese dried red chiles (see Note)

8 ounces air-dried, salt-cured pork belly or pancetta, thinly sliced into bite-size pieces (see Note)

Dark green parts from 2 large leeks, washed (see Prep Tip, page 64) and cut diagonally ½ inch thick

1 teaspoon sugar

1 tablespoon soy sauce

At Eric's, a Chinese restaurant near my home, owner Tony Sung makes a version of a Taiwanese stir-fry with cured pork belly and the dark green ends of leeks, a substitute for a particular kind of baby garlic shoots that are difficult to find here. It's a brilliant way to use a part of the leeks that usually gets thrown away. If you're not used to stir-frying with lots of whole chiles, start with five or ten, and turn on a fan because the fumes can make you cough. Serve with medium-grain rice.

Note: Chinese dried chiles, or Hunan chiles, are sold at Asian markets as is air-dried, salt-cured pork belly, such as Shin Tong Yan brand. If you can't find it, you can use pancetta instead, for a hybrid approach. (American-style salt pork is too salty.) At the deli counter, ask for pancetta sliced at least ¼ inch thick, then cut it into 1-inch strips.

Place a wok or large frying pan over medium heat and add the vegetable oil. When the oil is hot, add the garlic and chiles and stir-fry until fragrant, 3 to 4 minutes. Add the pork belly and stir-fry until the fat is translucent, about 3 minutes.

Tilt the wok to pour off all but 1 to 2 tablespoons of the fat. Add the leeks and stir-fry until tender, about 3 minutes.

Add the sugar and stir-fry for 1 minute more. Stir in the soy sauce and serve immediately.

LEEK GREENS & SHRIMP POT STICKERS MAKES 35 DUMPLINGS; SERVES 4 TO 6

Filling

1 tablespoon vegetable oil

2 cloves garlic, minced

1½ tablespoons finely chopped fresh ginger

1 large leek, white and green parts, washed (see Prep Tip, page 64), thinly sliced, and separated (1 to 2 cups leek greens)

Kosher salt

½ pound medium shrimp, peeled, deveined, and cut into ½-inch pieces

2 teaspoons toasted sesame oil

½ teaspoon sugar

35 wonton or other Asian dumpling wrappers (round or square)

1 to 2 tablespoons vegetable oil

Dipping sauce

¼ cup soy sauce

2 tablespoons cider vinegar or other sharp vinegar

2 tablespoons water

Chile oil

Shrimp and garlic chives are common fillings in Chinese dumplings, and here leek greens make an easy-to-find substitute for the chives. You use a whole leek in this recipe, plus extra leek greens you may have left from another recipe. The initial preparation is easy, but you may want to enlist a friend to help you assemble the pot stickers.

Note: To freeze, place uncooked pot stickers on a baking sheet lined with parchment paper, freeze until hard, and then store in zip-top bags for up to 2 months. There's no need to defrost them before cooking; just add a minute or two to the cooking time.

To make the filling, heat the vegetable oil with the garlic and ginger in a wok over medium heat until fragrant, 30 seconds. Add the leek greens, season lightly with salt, and stir-fry until wilted and partly tender, 2 to 3 minutes. Add the leek whites and cook until tender, another 2 to 3 minutes. Allow to cool to room temperature.

In a food processor, pulse the cooled leek greens mixture until chopped. Add the shrimp, sesame oil, sugar, and ½ teaspoon salt. Pulse 4 to 5 times until the mixture is combined but the shrimp is still chunky. Chill until cold, at least 30 minutes or up to overnight.

To assemble the pot stickers, place a wonton wrapper on a clean work surface. If the wrappers are square, place one with a corner pointing toward you. Dip a finger in water, then trace the margin of the top half of the wrapper. Add

→

a mounded teaspoonful of the filling to that half of the wrapper, leaving the margin uncovered. Fold the other half of the wrapper up and over the filling. Keeping the bottom flat at all times, make a pleat on the top half of wrapper and secure it to the bottom half (the water will help the pleat cling). If using round wrappers, first secure a pleat at the corner and then work your way around the sides. Create about 6 pleats per pot sticker until you have a sealed half-moon dumpling with a flat bottom. Repeat with the remaining pot stickers. Store in the refrigerator separated by layers of parchment paper to prevent sticking for up to 1 hour, or freeze at this point (see Note, page 68).

To make the dipping sauce, combine all of the sauce ingredients in a small serving bowl, adding the chile oil to taste.

To serve the pot stickers, place enough vegetable oil to liberally coat the bottom of a wok or nonstick skillet and place over medium heat. Add the pot stickers, flat side down, and cook, undisturbed, until golden, 1 to 2 minutes. Pour 1 to 2 tablespoons of water into the hot pan (beware of splattering), then cover, reduce the heat slightly, and steam until the water is gone and the filling is cooked through, 2 to 3 minutes.

Serve the pot stickers immediately with the dipping sauce alongside.

BEANS & LEEK GREENS SOUP SERVES 8 TO 10

Beans

- 1 pound dried beans, such as pinto, Great Northern, or cannellini beans, or a combination
- 2 stalks celery, halved, or leaves and inner stalks from 1 bunch, trimmed
- ½ onion, peeled (halve the onion through the core), or 1 leek, white part only
- 3 whole cloves garlic, peeled
- 2 bay leaves
- 1 tablespoon kosher salt

Soup

- 2 tablespoons olive oil
- 2 cups thinly sliced leek greens, washed (see Prep Tip, page 64)
- 1 cup thinly sliced leek whites
- 1 carrot, quartered lengthwise and thinly sliced
- 1 stalk celery or celery hearts, thinly sliced
- 2 teaspoons kosher salt
- Freshly ground pepper
- 1 to 2 tablespoons sherry vinegar or fresh lemon juice
- Crispy Fried Leek Greens (page 65; optional)

Leeks are both an aromatic oniony element and a leafy green in this silky pureed soup, made with freshly cooked beans and their flavorful broth. You can prepare the beans—which can be a mix of whatever you have in the pantry—up to two days before you make the soup.

Note: You will need 1 to 2 leeks for this recipe.

....

To prepare the beans, sort through to check for pebbles. Rinse the beans, place in a large pot, and cover with water by 2 inches. Either soak overnight or do a quick soak: bring to a rolling boil, then remove from the heat, cover, and let sit for 1 hour.

Drain the beans and return them to the pot. Fill the pot with enough water to cover the beans by at least 3 inches. Add the celery, onion, garlic, and bay leaves and bring to a simmer. Reduce to a low simmer and cook until the beans are tender, usually between 1 and 2 hours, depending on the type of beans and their freshness. Keep hot water on hand to maintain the water level, which helps the beans cook evenly.

When the beans are starting to get tender but are still a bit crunchy in the middle, about 20 minutes before they are done, add the salt.

Remove and discard the celery, onion, garlic, and bay leaves. (You can prepare the beans up to two days ahead. Let cool completely, then store in their cooking liquid, tightly covered, in the refrigerator.)

To make the soup, drain the beans, reserving the cooking liquid. Measure the cooking liquid and add water, if needed, so you have 6 cups. (If you have extra broth, store in the refrigerator or freezer for use in another soup.)

Add the olive oil to a stockpot and place over medium-low heat. Add the leek greens and whites, carrot, and celery. Sauté until the vegetables are tender and wilted, about 10 minutes. Add the beans and the 6 cups cooking liquid and bring to a simmer. Cook until the leek greens are very tender, about 10 minutes.

Using a blender or an immersion blender, puree the soup to the desired consistency, either a little chunky or very smooth. You may want to stir in another cup of bean broth, if you have it, or water. Season with 2 teaspoons salt, or to taste, and pepper to taste then stir in the vinegar or lemon juice. It will taste very acidic at first; let the soup sit for 5 minutes to give the vinegar a chance to mellow, then serve right away with the fried leek greens.

3

LEAVES

As we learned in grade school, leaves collect sunlight, turning it into food for the plant. In turn, our craving for leaves seems to be universal. In addition to the heaps of salads we go through, we are also growing to love heartier greens that require cooking, such as kale and chard, which aren't quite as easy to prepare but are delicious in their own sophisticated ways. We also eagerly buy up, and often grow, a wide variety of herbs to add freshness to home-cooked meals. Yet a lot of these leafy greens leave behind extras, such as the stems of kale or parsley and the dark outer leaves of romaine lettuce that are sacrificed in the name of a Caesar salad. This chapter provides ideas for how to use all of those parts, as well as how to tackle the extra half bunches of herbs and the ends of cabbage heads that often collect in the bottom of vegetable drawers.

Season: Most herbs and lettuces grow year round, though some varieties are seasonal. The main cabbage season is summer and early fall, though it can be grown most of the year in warmer climates.

Cabbage Rolls with Ginger Pork **80**

Sauerkraut **83**

Garlic-Braised Greens **87**

Chard Stalk Relish with Pine Nuts & Sultanas **89**

Chard Stalk Hummus **91**

Gialina's Kale & Farro Salad with Avocado **92**

Herb Salt **96**

Herb-Citrus Butter **98**

Basil-Lemon Pistou **99**

Rosemary Lard Butter **100**

Chimichurri **102**

Cilantro Chutney **103**

Chilaquiles with Cilantro Salsa & Queso Fresco **105**

Green Ceviche **106**

Cilantro Salsa **108**

Lemongrass Grilled Chicken **109**

Fattoush Salad **110**

Romaine Leaf Soup with Leeks & Peas **114**

Salmon with Whole Grilled Lettuce & Charred Tomatoes **115**

Romaine Wraps with Brown Rice & Bulgogi **116**

Cabbage

Prep Tip

To core and shred cabbage, first cut it into quarters (as pictured above), slicing through the stem end. Place each quarter on your work surface on one flat side and remove the core portion with a diagonal cut. You can shred it with thin cuts using a large, sharp knife, or use a food processor to shred it even more finely.

Because cabbage stores so well and is inexpensive, I often buy it and then neglect it for days or weeks at a time. One head of typical size is big enough to feed eight or ten people, so I usually end up with a half or a quarter of a cabbage that I eventually shred into a slaw with other crunchy vegetables, such as in the Celery Slaw with Apple Peel & Ginger Dressing (page 52). Or I'll wilt it with thinly sliced onions and apples, stock, and wine in a quick braise.

Lately I have turned most of my extra cabbage into sauerkraut, which is surprisingly easy to make (page 83). Even a relatively small amount of cabbage makes enough kraut to accompany simple meals of sausage and potatoes for weeks to come. You can also use the outer leaves and larger inner leaves of green cabbage as wrappers for almost anything, because they are sturdy enough for long steaming yet still look elegant when the dish is served. On page 80, you'll find a Polish-Chinese hybrid of cabbage leaves stuffed with ginger-flavored pork and rice, the translucent green leaves making pretty little bundles on the plate.

To store cabbage, keep it in a plastic bag in the refrigerator for 1 to 2 weeks.

CABBAGE ROLLS WITH GINGER PORK
MAKES 8 ROLLS; SERVES 4 AS A MAIN COURSE

Use any leftover cabbage in the Celery Slaw with Apple Peel & Ginger Dressing (page 52).

8 large green cabbage leaves, or 1 small head green cabbage

Filling

½ **cup uncooked jasmine rice**

½ **pound ground pork**

3 **tablespoons chopped water chestnuts**

3 **tablespoons minced green onions, white and green parts**

1 **to 2 tablespoons chopped cilantro**

2 **teaspoons minced fresh ginger**

1 **teaspoon finely minced garlic**

1½ **tablespoons soy sauce**

1 **tablespoon hoisin sauce**

1 **teaspoon rice vinegar**

Sauce

¼ **cup soy sauce**

2 **tablespoons rice vinegar**

2 **tablespoons water**

1 **to 2 teaspoons chili oil**

The love child of Polish stuffed cabbage and Chinese dumplings, this recipe uses up the large outer leaves of cabbage to wrap a rice-and-pork filling seasoned with ginger, cilantro, and soy sauce. Traditional stuffed cabbage recipes usually call for removing the spine from each leaf, but it's okay to leave them attached here. The sauce takes its cue from the dipping sauce usually served with pot stickers (page 68).

Note: If you don't have any leftover cabbage, you can also use large chard leaves. Cut off the stem at the bottom of each leaf and blanch in boiling water until softened, about 30 seconds.

....

Bring a large pot of water to boil. To remove the cabbage leaves, cut off the cabbage stem, and peel the leaves from the base. Blanch the leaves in the boiling water until just tender, about 2 minutes. Remove and let drain on clean kitchen towels. If the cabbage head is too tightly packed to remove the raw leaves without tearing them, place the whole head in the boiling water, core side down, and simmer for 3 minutes, covered. Drain the cabbage on a kitchen towel until cool. Cutting the leaves at the base to loosen them, gently remove them. Reserve any extra or torn leaves to line the steamer.

To make the filling, gently combine all of the filling ingredients in a large bowl.

Place a cabbage leaf on a clean work surface, cupped side facing up. Scoop up a portion of the filling using a ¼ cup measuring cup to shape it, then place the filling on the center of the leaf. Fold the bottom over the filling, then fold in the sides, then fold the top down. Place the rolls fold side down on a clean surface. (You can prepare the rolls to this point up to 4 hours in advance and keep them in the refrigerator, tightly wrapped.)

Set up a large steamer, such as a bamboo steamer or a large wire steamer, with plenty of water and line the rack with extra cabbage leaves. Place the cabbage rolls, folded side down, in the steamer and steam until the rice is fully cooked when you open one of the rolls to check, 30 to 40 minutes. (The rice can take up to 1 hour if the rolls are stacked or you have more than one level of racks in your steamer.) Remove the pan from the heat and let the rolls sit in the steamer for 5 to 10 minutes.

To make the sauce, stir together all of the sauce ingredients in a small serving bowl. Serve the rolls drizzled with the sauce.

SAUERKRAUT MAKES 3 TO 4 PINTS

2 pounds green cabbage

1½ tablespoons coarse sea salt or kosher salt

1 teaspoon caraway seeds (optional)

Most sauerkraut available at the store is made with a vinegar brine that turns the cabbage very sour and kind of chewy, but the real stuff is much more delicate, made with just cabbage and salt. I learned how easy it is to make during a class with Kathryn Lukas of Farmhouse Culture in Santa Cruz, California. When the shredded cabbage comes in contact with the salt, it draws out the vegetable's juices to create a pickling brine, which gives the finished kraut a more mild sourness. You can control the acidity to taste with the length of time you allow it to ferment at room temperature. The following recipe is a version of what Lukas taught me. Those who have a kitchen scale can make this recipe by using 1.5 percent salt compared to the weight of the cabbage.

Note: Sauerkraut takes about 2 weeks to ferment at room temperature. Once in the refrigerator, it will keep for several months. You will need 3 or 4 wide-mouth pint jars or 2 quart jars, plus their canning lids and rings, cleaned well in hot soapy water.

Remove a few large outer cabbage leaves and set aside to use as "lids" on the sauerkraut. Core and shred the cabbage (see Prep Tip, page 78). If shredding it by hand, try to make the pieces a consistent size.

Place the shredded cabbage in a large bowl with 1 tablespoon of the coarse sea salt or kosher salt. Using clean hands, massage the cabbage, grabbing it in clumps and squeezing it to work in the salt and tenderize it, until a brine starts to form. Let sit for 20 minutes. Squeeze some more to continue releasing the juices.

Add the caraway and taste; it should taste very salty. If not, add up to another ½ tablespoon salt. Fill a pint jar with the sauerkraut and, using your clean fist or a large spoon, pack the cabbage down as far as it will go, so it releases more liquid. Fill all the jars this way, leaving ½ inch at the top, then top each with a reserved cabbage leaf. Pour any brine in the bottom of the bowl on top of each jar; the sauerkraut should be covered by brine by ¼ inch. If it isn't, add a brine made of 1½ tablespoons kosher salt dissolved in 2 cups of water.

Cover the jars with the lids and close securely but not too tightly. Place the jars on plates in case they overflow during fermentation and store in a cool, dark spot, such as a kitchen cupboard. Often the sauerkraut brine leaks out of the jars (bubbling is natural); if that happens, add a little more brine to the jar. Let ferment for 10 days, then taste. If you like the flavor, place it in the refrigerator, which stops fermentation. If you'd like a more sour flavor, continue fermenting for another few days or a week. The sauerkraut will keep in the refrigerator for several months.

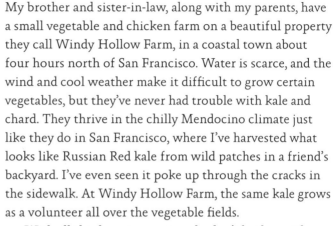

Chard and Kale

My brother and sister-in-law, along with my parents, have a small vegetable and chicken farm on a beautiful property they call Windy Hollow Farm, in a coastal town about four hours north of San Francisco. Water is scarce, and the wind and cool weather make it difficult to grow certain vegetables, but they've never had trouble with kale and chard. They thrive in the chilly Mendocino climate just like they do in San Francisco, where I've harvested what looks like Russian Red kale from wild patches in a friend's backyard. I've even seen it poke up through the cracks in the sidewalk. At Windy Hollow Farm, the same kale grows as a volunteer all over the vegetable fields.

With all this bounty, most cooks don't bother with kale or chard stalks, since they take longer to cook than the leaves. But you can also serve both kale stems and leaves raw, like chef Sharon Ardiana does partnered with farro and avocado in her delicious salad (page 92). And chard stems have a pleasant crunch and mild flavor that shouldn't always take a backseat to the leaves. In fact, in Europe the stems are served alone as their own vegetable.

Though they are often prepared in similar ways, kale and chard are members of different plant families. Kale is a cruciferous vegetable, which explains its bitter edge, while chard shares a botanical name with beets (*Beta vulgaris*) and is sweeter. You can buy bunches of green chard with white or red stems and veins, or rainbow chard, the marketing name for bunches of chard that have stems in different neon hues. I've never noticed much difference in flavor between different types of chard, whereas the different varieties of kale do have distinct qualities. The Russian Red kale that I've spotted growing wild has a frilly texture similar to that of curly kale, which is usually the one that is easiest to find in stores. My favorite is Tuscan kale, also known as Lacinato kale or dino kale—which you can spot by its narrow and leathery-looking dark

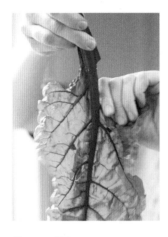

Prep Tip

To remove stems from chard or kale, start by trimming the stem ends. Then hold a leaf by the stem in one hand and use the other hand to tear the leaves from the stem into bite-size pieces. To make cleaner-looking stems, use a knife to cut the leaves from the stem on both sides in a pointy triangle.

green leaves—for its silkier texture, bright color, and deep flavor, but even the kind growing out of sidewalk cracks is delicious.

Store bunches of greens in plastic bags in the refrigerator for no more than 3 to 5 days for best flavor. After removing the stems from the greens, you can store both in plastic bags for 2 to 3 days.

GARLIC-BRAISED GREENS SERVES 2 TO 4

If you don't use the stems here, use them in the Chard Stalk Relish with Pine Nuts & Sultanas (page 89) or the Chard Stalk Hummus (page 91).

2 bunches kale or chard, stemmed (see Prep Tip, page 85)

2 tablespoons extra-virgin olive oil, plus more for drizzling

3 whole cloves garlic, peeled and crushed with the side of a knife

⅛ teaspoon red chile flakes

Kosher salt

Juice of ½ lemon

This is a building block recipe for cooking chard or kale as a side dish for meats or fish, or as a base for a pasta sauce. You can chose to add the stems to the braise, or keep them for another recipe. Just toss the greens into a pan sizzling with garlic, red chile flakes, and olive oil and steam them until fully tender.

Note: Turnip greens, beet greens, kohlrabi greens, collards, mustard greens, and pea shoots all work using this method.

Wash the greens and leave wet. Tear the leaves into bite-size pieces and slice the stems, if using, ¼ inch thick; keep the leaves and stems separate. (If you'd like to use the greens in a pasta, cut the leaves into 1-inch dice so that they will better coat the pasta.)

Heat the olive oil in a wok or large skillet over medium heat. Add the garlic and red chile flakes and swirl in the hot oil until fragrant, about 30 seconds. Add the stems and stir-fry for 1 minute, then cover and cook with a splash of water until mostly tender, 6 to 8 minutes.

Add a few handfuls of the leaves and stir, adding more as they wilt. After you've added about one-third, sprinkle with salt to help the greens shrink and be seasoned evenly. When all the leaves are wilted, add a splash of water (unless the greens were very wet). Cover, reduce the heat to low, and cook until tender, 3 to 5 minutes for chard and 8 to 10 minutes for kale.

Season with salt and lemon juice. Place in a serving bowl and drizzle with olive oil. Serve hot or at room temperature.

CHARD STALK RELISH WITH PINE NUTS & SULTANAS SERVES 4

Use the chard leaves in Garlic-Braised Greens (page 87).

⅓ cup golden raisins, currants, or raisins

2 tablespoons sherry vinegar or red wine vinegar

2 tablespoons water

¼ cup pine nuts

2 tablespoons extra-virgin olive oil

½ cup finely diced red onion

Large pinch of red chile flakes, or 1 small dried red chile, crumbled

½ teaspoon minced garlic

Stalks from 1 large bunch chard, preferably rainbow chard, removed with a knife (see Prep Tip, page 85), and sliced ¼ inch thick

Kosher salt

When you have leftover stalks from a bunch or two of chard, you can chop them, sauté them until tender, then toss them with golden raisins (sultanas) and toasted pine nuts to make a tangy relish for pork, lamb, or firm fish like swordfish. With its vinegar-soaked raisins, the relish even works as a creative substitute for cranberry relish at holiday dinners if you double or triple the recipe.

Note: Slivered almonds can substitute for the pine nuts.

Place the golden raisins in a small bowl with the vinegar and water. Let soak while you prepare the other ingredients.

Place the pine nuts in a small frying pan over medium-low heat. Toast, tossing occasionally, until golden, about 6 minutes. Watch carefully, as they burn easily. Transfer to a plate and let cool.

Place 1 tablespoon of the olive oil in a sauté pan over medium heat. Add the onion and red chile flakes and sauté, stirring occasionally, until the onion is mostly tender, about 5 minutes. Add the garlic and chard stalks and cook for about 2 minutes. Add a splash of water, cover, and cook, stirring occasionally, until the stalks are tender, about 10 minutes.

→

Add the sultanas with their soaking liquid and bring to a simmer. Allow the liquid to cook off slightly, about 1 minute. Remove from the heat, stir in the pine nuts and the remaining 1 tablespoon olive oil, and season to taste with salt. Serve immediately or at room temperature.

You can hold the relish for up to 3 days in the refrigerator. Bring to room temperature and add the toasted pine nuts right before serving.

CHARD STALK HUMMUS MAKES 1 CUP

Chard stalks from 1 pound whole chard, trimmed and chopped (see Prep Tip, page 85)

1 whole clove garlic, peeled

¼ cup tahini

¼ cup extra-virgin olive oil, plus more for drizzling

2 tablespoons fresh lemon juice

½ teaspoon kosher salt

In the Mediterranean, chard stalks are used in place of chickpeas to make a dip that is similar to hummus, with tahini, garlic, lemon, and olive oil. Paula Wolfert's *The Cooking of the Eastern Mediterranean* and Clifford Wright's *Mediterranean Vegetables* both include recipes for it. Here is my version of this creamy spread, which you can serve with any type of flatbread.

Bring a large pot of water to boil and cook the stalks until very tender, 18 to 20 minutes. Drain.

Place the garlic in a food processor and pulse until chopped. Add the chard stalks and puree, then add the remaining ingredients and process until very smooth.

Transfer to a shallow bowl, drizzle with olive oil, and serve at room temperature. The hummus also can be stored in the refrigerator for up to 3 days. Return to room temperature before serving.

GIALINA'S KALE & FARRO SALAD WITH AVOCADO SERVES 6 TO 8

Dressing

1 stalk green garlic, white and light green parts, chopped, or 2 cloves garlic, chopped

Leaves from ½ bunch tarragon

Leaves from ½ bunch Italian parsley

1½ cups extra-virgin olive oil

½ cup Moscatel vinegar (see Note)

1 tablespoon Dijon mustard

1 teaspoon kosher salt

¼ teaspoon freshly ground pepper

Salad

⅔ cup farro

1 bunch Tuscan kale (about 10 ounces)

1 to 2 avocados, cut into large dice

2 spring carrots, peeled or scrubbed and sliced into thin rounds

Kosher salt and freshly ground pepper

Our neighborhood pizzeria, Gialina, gets high marks for its thin-crust pies and the impeccable produce that chef-owner Sharon Ardiana uses in her toppings and sides. Her salads are always irresistible, and this one is not only delicious, it also uses whole kale leaves, including the stems. Ardiana tosses chopped raw kale with bright rounds of sweet carrots, creamy avocado, and a handful of nutty farro for sweetness and texture, and then adds a garlic dressing that is reminiscent of green goddess dressing but without the mayonnaise.

Note: Ardiana's favorite vinegar, and mine too, is Moscatel vinegar made by the Spanish brand Unio. It's spendy but complex and fruity. Look for it online or at Whole Foods or specialty stores, or substitute Champagne vinegar or white wine vinegar. You only need half to two-thirds of the dressing for this recipe; leftovers will hold for about a week in the refrigerator.

To make the dressing, place all of the dressing ingredients in a blender or food processor and blend until smooth, or use an immersion blender to blend all the ingredients in a bowl.

To make the salad, bring a small pot of salted water to a boil. Add the farro and cook until tender, 16 to 18 minutes. Drain, rinse with cold water until cool, then drain well.

Remove the stems from the kale (see Prep Tip, page 85). Cut away any tough ends, then finely slice the stems and

tear the kale leaves into small bite-size pieces. Place both the stems and leaves in a large salad bowl. Add the avocados, carrots, and farro. Add half of the dressing and toss to combine. Add more dressing if desired. Season to taste with salt and pepper and serve.

Herbs

Of all the fresh produce in a home cook's repertoire, fresh herbs are the ones we worry about wasting the most. After a few sprigs go into a recipe, they tend to get stuffed in a bag and stowed deep in the refrigerator. You can prolong the life of herbs by chopping them and then preserving them in fat or acid, such as lemon or lime juice, or in a combination of both, which is the idea behind many of the recipes that follow, including the Herb-Citrus Butter (page 98), Rosemary Lard Butter (page 100), Cilantro Chutney (page 103), Cilantro Salsa (page 108), Basil-Lemon Pistou (page 99), and Chimichurri (page 102). And my Carrot Top Salsa Verde (page 34) works made with extra parsley and other herbs, too.

You can also use tender herbs like parsley and cilantro in salads, turning their leaves into tender greens, such as in the Middle Eastern Fattoush Salad (page 110). Or simply grind up the herbs with flake salt (page 96) and leave the mixture to dry, preserving them for weeks to come.

You can also wrap unwashed herbs in damp paper towels, place in a plastic bag, and keep in the refrigerator for 3 days to 1 week.

HERB SALT MAKES ¾ CUP

½ cup fresh thyme,
rosemary, sage, or
oregano leaves, or a
combination

2 tablespoons plus ½ cup
kosher or flaky sea salt

Making herb salt is one of the easiest ways to preserve excess herbs, and it also makes an excellent gift. You just pulse the herbs in a spice grinder with salt, then spread the mixture out to dry before putting it in jars. If you are not bagging it to give away to friends, rub the salt on pork roasts, whole chickens, fish, or steaks, sprinkle it over roasted potatoes, or whisk it into vinaigrettes or other sauces.

Note: Some food processors have a tough time breaking down soft fresh herbs, especially rosemary, which is why I suggest using a spice grinder.

Combine the herbs with the 2 tablespoons salt in a spice grinder and pulse until the herbs are finely chopped. Transfer to a medium bowl, combine with the remaining ½ cup salt, and stir until combined.

Spread the salt on a rimmed baking sheet and let dry for 4 to 8 hours at room temperature. The salt will store, tightly covered, for at least three months.

HERB-CITRUS BUTTER MAKES ¾ CUP

3 tablespoons finely minced fresh herbs, such as tarragon, rosemary, Italian parsley, basil, cilantro, oregano, and sage

1 tablespoon finely grated (with a Microplane) lemon or other citrus zest

1 teaspoon fresh lemon, lime, or grapefruit juice

1 tablespoon finely minced shallots

Kosher salt and freshly ground pepper

½ cup unsalted butter, at room temperature

This recipe keeps herbs fresh by combining them with butter. Roll the compound butter into a log and chill it in the fridge or freezer, then slice off a few thin discs to garnish broiled fish, hot grilled steak, or corn on the cob. As the butter melts, it spreads herby love all over. Or rub the herb butter over a whole chicken you're going to roast, tucking some under the skin on the breasts and thighs. You can also toss it with cooked vegetables or melt it into a dipping sauce for artichokes or shellfish.

Note: Try to use a mix of both mild and strongly flavored herbs, if possible. If you have any flowering herbs, throw in some of the buds for a bit of color.

Place all of the ingredients in a medium bowl and beat with a wooden spoon until combined. Place the mixture on a sheet of plastic wrap and roll into a log 1 inch in diameter. Wrap tightly with the plastic wrap, twist the ends closed, and store in the refrigerator for up to 2 weeks or in the freezer for up to 2 months.

If frozen, allow the log to defrost for 15 to 30 minutes before slicing off what you need and returning the rest to the freezer.

BASIL-LEMON PISTOU MAKES 1 CUP

1 whole clove garlic, peeled

1 teaspoon grated lemon zest

2 teaspoons fresh lemon juice, or to taste

2 cups basil leaves

¼ teaspoon kosher salt

½ cup extra-virgin olive oil, plus more as needed

Pistou, a French basil-garlic sauce, is the predecessor of pesto, which comes from Italy's Ligurian coast on the French border. Although it sometimes contains pine nuts and Parmesan, here it's made without, which makes it simple to pull together when you have extra basil to use up. I also added lemon juice and zest for a slightly brighter flavor—and to provide another outlet for extra citrus. Traditionally swirled into a vegetable-bean soup or served over pasta or with roast lamb, pistou also works in vinaigrettes, on sandwiches, or as a dipping sauce or bruschetta topping.

. . . .

Place the garlic and lemon zest in a food processor (a small one will work) and pulse until chopped. Add the lemon juice and basil and puree until chopped. Add the salt and then add the olive oil in a slow drizzle while processing until combined. Pour into a container and top with additional oil to cover all of the basil (this prevents the pistou from browning). Serve at room temperature.

The sauce will hold for 1 week, tightly covered, in the refrigerator, or 1 month in the freezer.

ROSEMARY LARD BUTTER MAKES ⅔ CUP

A jewel box of a butcher shop near our house, Avedano's, has all kinds of surprises in its meat case, including what it calls lard butter. The butchers run pork fat through a meat grinder a few times to make a incredible spread with rosemary and garlic. What's not to like? In this homage, you can use fat you've collected from cooking bacon or other types of pork, or you can render pork fat—either scraps from trimming a pork roast or fat purchased from a butcher shop. The hot liquid is then poured over chopped rosemary and garlic. After it cools and thickens, you have a luscious spread to serve with a fresh baguette.

4 ounces pork fat, cut into ¼-inch cubes, or about ⅔ cup rendered lard or bacon fat

2 cloves garlic, minced

2 teaspoons chopped fresh rosemary

Kosher salt

Note: If the idea of eating room temperature lard doesn't appeal, use the lard butter to make porky bruschetta. Just spread a thin layer of lard butter on thick slices of day-old country bread and grill over medium heat for 2 minutes per side.

If using solid pork fat, to render the fat, you can either cook the ¼-inch cubes directly or first pulse the fat in a food processor until chunky (this method yields more liquid fat). Place the fat in a medium sauté pan over medium-low heat and cook until it has rendered into liquid and the cracklings in the pan are crisp and lightly browned, 10 to 15 minutes. If using bacon fat or lard that has already been rendered, heat it in a sauté pan over medium heat until liquid.

Place the garlic, rosemary, and ½ teaspoon salt (or less if using bacon fat) in a half-pint canning jar and set a fine mesh-strainer on top. Pour the hot fat through the strainer into the bowl. (If you started with solid fat, you will have cracklings left to garnish other dishes.) Stir to dissolve the salt and let the lard butter sit at room temperature until cool. Close the lid and refrigerate until solid, several hours or overnight.

Stir the lard butter before serving. The lard butter will hold for 2 weeks in an airtight container in the refrigerator, or 1 month in the freezer.

CHIMICHURRI MAKES 1 CUP

½ cup extra-virgin olive oil

¼ cup red wine vinegar

½ cup finely chopped Italian parsley leaves and tender stems

2 tablespoons finely chopped fresh oregano

¼ cup finely diced red onion

2 cloves garlic, minced

½ teaspoon kosher salt

A fresh herb sauce from Argentina traditionally served with meats and empanadas, chimichurri is one of my favorite uses for extra parsley and oregano. Its combination of sharp, pungent, and fresh flavors, rounded out by rich olive oil, makes it irresistible with simply seasoned steaks right off the grill.

Combine all of the ingredients in a small bowl and stir until the salt dissolves. Let sit for about 20 minutes to allow the flavors to meld, then serve at room temperature.

The sauce will hold for 1 week, tightly covered, in the refrigerator.

CILANTRO CHUTNEY MAKES 1 CUP

1 bunch cilantro

2 large whole cloves garlic, peeled

1 serrano chile, seeded and quartered

½ cup water

¼ cup fresh lemon juice

1 tablespoon sugar

2 teaspoons finely grated fresh ginger

½ teaspoon kosher salt

Both Indian and Mexican cuisines have everyday sauces made of chopped cilantro, chiles, and garlic. In Mexico, the sauce, which also contains tomatillos, is called salsa verde (page 108), while in India, it's cilantro chutney. Chutney is sweeter, with ginger, a bit of sugar, and usually some mint, too. This version is an easy way to use up extra cilantro, including some of the stems, and so refreshing and bright that you might start adding it to everything—panini, roast meats, even burritos—not just curry and samosas. If you prefer a hotter chutney, leave in the seeds from the chile.

Note: Mint leaves can be substituted for some of the cilantro.

Remove the bottom third of the stems from the cilantro bunches and discard, then coarsely chop the remaining cilantro and stems.

Place the garlic and chile in a blender or food processor and pulse until finely chopped. (A blender will produce a smoother sauce.) Add the cilantro, water, lemon juice, sugar, ginger, and salt and pulse until a chunky sauce forms, scraping down the sides a few times. Serve at room temperature.

The sauce will hold for 5 days, tightly covered, in the refrigerator.

CHILAQUILES WITH CILANTRO SALSA & QUESO FRESCO SERVES 2

¼ cup vegetable oil

6 (6-inch) corn tortillas, each cut into 6 wedges, or about 4 cups thick-cut tortilla chips

1 cup Cilantro Salsa (page 108)

½ cup crumbled queso fresco

Mexico is responsible for some of the world's most delicious breakfasts, and chilaquiles stands among the best of them. You take fried tortilla wedges—a thrifty use for stale tortillas—and cook them with salsa just long enough to soak up the sauce but stay crisp. If you can't be bothered to fry tortillas in the early morning hours, you can purchase thick-cut tortilla chips made from real tortillas (not mass-produced Doritos-type chips). Serve with scrambled or fried eggs on the side.

To pan-fry the tortillas, heat the vegetable oil in a medium skillet over medium-high heat. When the oil is hot enough to bubble when you dip a tortilla in it, place about one third of the tortillas in a single layer and cook until lightly browned and crisp (though not as crisp as tortilla chips), 1 to 2 minutes per side. Use a slotted spoon to transfer to paper towels to drain, then repeat with the remaining tortillas.

Drain all but a thin layer of oil from the pan and reduce the heat to medium. Add the salsa and heat briefly until warmed through, then add the fried tortillas or tortilla chips. Toss to coat until the tortillas have absorbed some of the sauce but are still crisp, 1 to 2 minutes (if you are using very crunchy tortilla chips, cook a few minutes longer). Remove from the heat, sprinkle with the cheese, and serve immediately.

GREEN CEVICHE SERVES 2 TO 4

½ pound very fresh firm white fish (see Note), cut into cubes ¼ inch or smaller

5 to 6 tablespoons fresh lime juice (from 3 to 4 limes)

¾ teaspoon kosher salt

½ cup Cilantro Salsa (page 108)

Tostadas or thick-cut tortilla chips

1 ripe avocado, sliced

Hot sauce

This dish provides another use for the Cilantro Salsa (page 108), and it's also not a bad way to use up an extra fish fillet (as long as it's super-fresh), since a little goes a long way. My husband and I got hooked on ceviche after a trip to Ensenada, a fishing port on Mexico's Baja Peninsula, where raw fish is served in many different forms. Though I have tried making it with different types of salsa, I really like the herbal notes you get from the cilantro, tomatillos, and green chiles in the Cilantro Salsa.

Note: Use the highest-quality, freshest ocean-caught fish you can find, such as Pacific snapper, Pacific sea bass, wild salmon, or halibut. For the best texture, cut the fish into small, uniform cubes with a sharp knife.

Place the fish in a small bowl with enough lime juice to cover generously. Stir in the salt. Refrigerate for 20 minutes to 1 hour; the longer the fish marinates the firmer and more acidic it will become, so prepare it the way you prefer.

Stir in the salsa, return to the refrigerator, and let sit another 15 to 30 minutes.

Serve the ceviche very cold, in a bowl next to the tostadas, avocado, and hot sauce. I like to smear avocado on the tostada and then top it with the ceviche and a few squirts of hot sauce.

CILANTRO SALSA MAKES ABOUT 2 CUPS

Based on Mexican salsa verde, which is different from the Italian sauce of the same name (page 34), this sauce is packed with fresh tomatillos, onion, and fresh green chiles. This version uses some of the cilantro stems and makes use of half an avocado, if you happen to have one. It comes out with the perfect consistency for the Chilaquiles with Cilantro Salsa & Queso Fresco (page 105) or the Green Ceviche (page 106).

Note: I prefer to leave in the seeds from the jalapeño or serrano when making this salsa, which will taste spicy at first but will mellow as it sits. Remove the seeds if you prefer a milder sauce.

1 whole clove garlic, peeled

1 jalapeño or serrano chile, quartered

12 ounces fresh tomatillos, husked, rinsed, and halved

1 cup packed coarsely chopped cilantro leaves and tender stems

1 cup coarsely chopped white onion

½ teaspoon kosher salt

½ ripe avocado (optional)

½ cup water (optional)

Place the garlic and chile in a food processor and pulse until chopped. Add the tomatillos, cilantro, onion, salt, and avocado. Pulse until evenly chopped but still chunky, stirring a few times to scrape down the sides of the bowl.

To use in chilaquiles or ceviche, leave as is. To serve as a dip with chips, stir in ½ cup water. Let sit at room temperature for at least 30 minutes before serving to let the flavors develop.

The sauce will hold for 5 days, tightly covered, in the refrigerator.

LEMONGRASS GRILLED CHICKEN SERVES 4

The lemongrass shoots can be used in the Thai Watermelon Salad with Crunchy Watermelon Rind (page 187).

Marinade

- 2 stalks lemongrass, trimmed and bulbs finely chopped (about ⅓ cup)

- 1 shallot, finely chopped (about ¼ cup)

- 2 cloves garlic, minced

- 2 tablespoons Asian fish sauce

- 2 tablespoons soy sauce

- 2 tablespoons vegetable oil

- 1 tablespoon dark brown sugar

- 2 pounds bone-in chicken parts

Prep Tip

To trim lemongrass, remove the bottoms and thin top parts of the shoot, then finely chop the bulbous part on the bottom.

If you ever experiment with Southeast Asian cooking, you're likely to have leftover lemongrass, which holds for some time in the refrigerator, maintaining its fragrance much longer than leafy herbs do. When you find yourself with some, make a batch of this easy lemongrass marinade, which is versatile enough to use on tofu or any kind of grilled meat, including boneless or bone-in chicken, pork, or beef. You can also roast the chicken in a baking dish in a 400°F oven for 30 to 45 minutes, or until cooked through. Serve with rice.

To make the marinade, combine all of the marinade ingredients in a large bowl. Toss with the chicken, cover, and marinate in the refrigerator for at least 1 hour or overnight before grilling.

Preheat a grill to medium heat (350° to 450°F). Grill the chicken, turning often, until cooked through to the bone, 30 to 45 minutes (thighs take the longest). Let cool for 10 minutes before serving.

FATTOUSH SALAD SERVES 4

Use the dark green outer leaves from the romaine lettuce in the Romaine Leaf Soup with Leeks and Peas (page 114) or the Romaine Wraps with Brown Rice & Bulgogi (page 116).

Fattoush is a traditional salad from the Mediterranean made with whole tender herbs; here you can use a mix of whatever you have. It's also a good way to revive stale pita bread, which becomes toasty and crisp in the oven, just like when you make croutons with a day-old baguette. This recipe uses ground sumac, a lemony-flavored purple berry, and pomegranate syrup, a sweet-tart condiment. Both are available in Middle Eastern stores and well-stocked grocery stores, but the salad is also fine without them.

2 pita bread rounds

2 teaspoons olive oil

Kosher salt

Dressing

2 teaspoons fresh lemon juice, plus more to taste

1 teaspoon pomegranate molasses, or ½ teaspoon honey

1 clove garlic, chopped

½ teaspoon sumac (optional)

⅛ teaspoon kosher salt

Freshly ground pepper

¼ cup olive oil, plus more to taste

Salad

1 romaine heart (see Prep Tip, page 113), cut into ribbons (about 4 cups)

½ English cucumber, halved lengthwise and thinly sliced

1 large tomato, diced, or 1 cup halved cherry tomatoes

2 green onions, white and half of green part, thinly sliced

Leaves from 5 sprigs Italian parsley, torn if large

Leaves from 5 sprigs mint, torn if large

Leaves from 5 sprigs cilantro (optional)

Kosher salt and freshly ground pepper

½ cup crumbled feta cheese

→

Preheat the oven to 350°F. Brush the pita on both sides with the olive oil, then cut into 2 by 1-inch strips. Place on a baking sheet, season with salt, and toast until crisp, 5 to 10 minutes, depending on how fresh the pita is (fresher bread takes longer to crisp up). Let cool in the pan.

To make the dressing, whisk together the lemon juice, pomegranate molasses, garlic, sumac, salt, and pepper to taste in a small bowl. Whisk in the olive oil, then adjust the seasoning to taste.

To make the salad, place the lettuce, cucumber, tomato, green onions, parsley, mint, and cilantro in a salad bowl with the pita croutons. Toss with the dressing and salt and pepper to taste, adding more olive oil and lemon juice if needed to bring the flavors together. Sprinkle the feta on top and serve immediately.

Romaine Lettuce

Prep Tip

To trim a head of romaine lettuce to the heart, chop off the top 2 inches of the greens and remove the outer dark green leaves until you get to the inner light green heart. Remove the stem (unless you are making the Romaine Leaf Soup on page 114).

I love Caesar salads, but I am not a big fan of the romaine hearts that come in a sealed bag, already stripped of their dark outer leaves. They're convenient, but the pale, antiseptic leaves are all crunch and no flavor, not unlike the iceberg lettuce of yore. I'd rather buy a whole head of romaine, but that does leave me with all those dark outer leaves.

Instead of throwing out the dark part, or suffering through them in my salad, I have started cooking them instead. They're perfect in soup made with the classic pairing of lettuce and peas (page 114), or prepared on the grill with a oil and vinegar marinade, served next to grilled salmon and tomatoes (page 115). I also love using them as fresh wrappers for Korean-style barbecue beef, or *bulgogi* (page 116). Hot off the grill, the garlicky beef melts into the fillings of rice, cucumbers, and chile sauce, with the crunchy lettuce surrounding it all.

Keep unwashed lettuce heads wrapped in damp paper towels inside a plastic bag for 3 to 5 days, refrigerated. Outer romaine leaves and dark parts will store the same way for several days.

ROMAINE LEAF SOUP WITH LEEKS & PEAS SERVES 8

2 tablespoons unsalted butter

2 small leeks or 1 large leek, washed (see Prep Tip, page 64) and thinly sliced

8 to 10 ounces dark green outer leaves, tops, and stalks from 1 large head romaine lettuce (see Prep Tip, page 113), stalks separated and coarsely chopped

2 quarts Vegetable Scraps Stock (page 10), or 1 quart purchased vegetable or chicken broth plus 1 quart water

1 cup frozen peas

Kosher salt and freshly ground pepper

½ cup plain yogurt, sour cream, or heavy cream

The dark green outer leaves from a head of romaine lettuce are delicious in a soup, creating a grassy, earthy puree that tastes similar to spinach or stinging nettles. The peas, which I usually can find tucked away in my freezer, smooth out the flavor and boost the color, and you can use whole leeks, greens and all. If you like, garnish the soup with croutons—made with leftover bread, of course.

Note: This recipe uses up the crunchy white stalks that run down the middle of the romaine leaves and even the stem, parts of the romaine lettuce that usually get thrown out. Just chop up these crunchy parts and cook them with the leeks before you add the leaves.

....

Heat the butter in a Dutch oven over medium heat and add the leeks, including the dark green parts, and the romaine stalks. Sauté, stirring occasionally, until very tender, about 12 minutes. Add the stock, bring to a simmer, and cook until the vegetables are soft and don't provide much resistance, about 15 minutes (make sure the leek greens are fully cooked). Add the romaine leaves and peas, return to a simmer, and cook for 8 minutes.

Using an immersion blender or regular blender in batches, puree the soup until very smooth. Season well with salt and pepper; you may need 2 or 3 teaspoons of salt if using an unsalted homemade stock. Reheat on low heat and stir in the yogurt. Serve immediately.

SALMON WITH WHOLE GRILLED LETTUCE & CHARRED TOMATOES SERVES 4

1 large head romaine lettuce, trimmed, washed, and patted dry

3 tablespoons olive oil

1 tablespoon sherry vinegar or red wine vinegar

½ teaspoon kosher salt

⅛ teaspoon freshly ground pepper

4 ripe Early Girl or Roma tomatoes

1½ pounds salmon fillets, pin bones removed

Grilled foods are often paired with salads for an appealing combination of hot, charred protein and fresh, crunchy leaves. In this case, you grill the salad, too, by quartering a whole romaine head, including the dark, slightly bitter outer leaves, until wilted and charred. It's delicious with grilled salmon and soft, sweet chunks of grilled tomatoes.

Note: You can substitute a head of red leaf or other sturdy lettuce, cut in half and grilled for about 5 minutes.

Preheat a grill to medium heat (350° to 450°F) and brush the grates well.

Quarter the romaine head through the core and place in a shallow dish. Drizzle with 1½ tablespoons of the olive oil and the vinegar. Season with a pinch of salt and pepper. Lightly coat the Roma tomatoes with ½ tablespoon of the olive oil. Season the salmon with ½ teaspoon salt and ⅛ teaspoon pepper, then coat with the remaining 1 tablespoon olive oil.

Place the salmon skin side down on the grill over direct heat. Place the lettuce wedges and tomatoes on a cooler part of the grill and cover the grill. Cook the salmon until still slightly dark in the middle, 7 to 8 minutes, turning once. Turn the vegetables every few minutes until the tomatoes have softened, 8 to 10 minutes, and the lettuce is crisp and brown (watch carefully to prevent burning), about 12 minutes.

Quarter the tomatoes and divide among four plates, seasoning them with salt and pepper. Distribute the lettuce wedges and salmon among the plates and serve immediately.

ROMAINE WRAPS WITH BROWN RICE & BULGOGI SERVES 4 TO 6

Bulgogi

- ¼ **cup water**
- 2 **tablespoons dark soy sauce**
- 2 **tablespoons light soy sauce**
- 1 **tablespoon dark brown sugar**
- 1 **tablespoon toasted sesame oil**
- 3 **green onions, white and half of green part, very thinly sliced, plus more for garnish**
- 1½ **tablespoons minced garlic**
- 12 **ounces boneless rib-eye or top round steak, very thinly sliced**

Fans of Korean barbecue are familiar with the idea of wrapping pieces of lettuce around thin slices of marinated grilled beef and rice for magic little bites that combine hot rice, blackened steak, and fresh, cold lettuce. It turns out that the outer leaves of romaine are perfect for the job. Traditional Korean barbecue restaurants put grills in the center of each table, and while you may not want to repeat that part at home, you can keep the interactive theme going. Place a plate of just-grilled steak in the center of the table, surrounded by bowls of rice, slivers of juicy cucumber, squirt bottles of chile sauce, and a platter of romaine for wrapping.

Note: Dark soy sauce is available at Korean and other Asian markets. Korean markets also sell very thinly sliced boneless beef for bulgogi, *or ask your butcher to slice your steak about ⅛ inch thick. You can do it yourself if you freeze the meat briefly first to firm it up. A little beef goes a long way in this recipe, but you can increase the quantity to 1 pound for hearty appetites; there's enough marinade.*

To make the bulgogi, combine the water, soy sauces, sugar, and sesame oil in a shallow baking dish just large enough to fit the beef and whisk until the sugar dissolves. Stir in the green onions and garlic, then add the steak, tossing to coat the slices evenly. Cover and marinate in the refrigerator for at least 4 hours, and preferably overnight.

To serve

Outer leaves from 1 large head romaine lettuce (about 6 to 8 leaves), or a combination of inner and outer leaves, cut into 4-inch pieces

2 cups cooked medium- or short-grained brown rice (from about 1 cup uncooked)

½ English cucumber, julienned

Red chile sauce

Toasted nori (pressed seaweed) squares, each 3 to 4 inches (optional)

To serve, preheat a grill or grill pan to medium-high heat (around 450°F). Soak the romaine in cold water to crisp, then pat dry with a clean kitchen towel. Place the romaine and the other serving ingredients in bowls on the table. Grill the beef until just cooked through, about 30 seconds to 1 minute per side. Serve immediately, instructing diners to wrap pieces of beef in the lettuce wrappers with some of the rice, cucumber, chile sauce, and reserved green onions. Nori squares can be used as alternative wrappers to augment the lettuce.

FLOWERS

It sounds romantic to eat flowers, yet that's exactly what we do anytime we eat cauliflower, broccoli, or artichokes. As flowers, or flower buds, they are part of a plant's reproductive system. In stores, broccoli and cauliflower are often sold hacked down to the florets, as if their stalks and leaves were worthless. Yet pretrimmed vegetables sacrifice a lot of their sweetness, leaving behind more of their sulfurous qualities. Whole broccoli is likely to be tastier, and you'll get a better yield if you just peel the stalks and add them to what you're cooking. The same holds true for cauliflower, which has a large inner stalk and many edible leaves. And if you trim artichokes down to their hearts, you're left with lots of leaves. The following pages offer ideas of what to do with all of these extras.

Season: Both cauliflower and broccoli are available year round, with a peak season during cooler months. The main season for artichokes is in the spring, with another smaller harvest in the fall. Squash blossoms are usually available in spring and summer.

Roasted Artichoke Leaves **123**

Fontina-Stuffed Squash Blossom Fritters **125**

Shaved Broccoli Stalk Salad with Lime & Cotija **129**

Golden Broccoli Spears with Tangerine Peel **130**

Broccoli Stalk Orecchiette with Anchovies & Garlic Bread Crumbs **131**

Pan-Roasted Cauliflower Steaks with Tomatoes & Capers **135**

Cauliflower with Smoked Paprika & Whole Wheat Linguine **136**

Broiled Cauliflower Steaks with Mustard Glaze **139**

Artichokes

A thistle covered in spiky leaves, the artichoke is one of nature's most intimidating edible plants. Only the heart plus a small portion of the leaves and stem are edible, and most people just cook the whole artichoke and then eat it, leaf by leaf. But for recipes that call for trimming artichokes down to the heart for pasta, antipasto, or an entrée like the Asparagus, Artichoke & Chickpea Ragout (page 49), there's a lot of waste. Yet it's actually not difficult to cook the excess outer leaves separately as an appetizer (as in the recipe opposite). The best way to avoid waste is to seek out smaller artichokes, usually called baby artichokes, which often don't have a choke and have fewer dark green outer leaves. When trimming an artichoke, keep in mind that any part that is dark green will be fibrous and inedible, while the light green parts, including the light green inner leaves, are edible.

Wrapped in a damp paper towel and stored in a plastic bag, artichokes will hold in the refrigerator for 2 to 3 days. After you trim artichokes, the excess leaves must be kept in a mixture of water and lemon juice and cooked right away to prevent them from browning.

Prep Tip

To trim artichoke hearts, first prepare a bowl of acidulated water by squeezing the juice of ½ lemon into a bowl of water. Use the remaining lemon half to rub on any cut surfaces of the artichokes as you trim them. Discard the artichoke's stem or carefully trim it down to its light green center and trim off any spikes. Cut off the top about 1 inch from the end, then remove the large, dark outer leaves until you get to the light green or yellow inner leaves. If you plan to use the leaves in the Roasted Artichoke Leaves (page 123), grasp with your thumb pressed at the base of each leaf so that more of the edible part stays attached to each leaf.

Trim the base, or bottom, of the artichoke down to the light green part. Quarter the cores, rubbing with lemon, and keep any cut parts in the acidulated water. Remove the choke attached to each quarter heart and any spiky inner leaves; the remaining pale green leaves are edible.

ROASTED ARTICHOKE LEAVES SERVES 2

This dish is meant to be a byproduct of trimming artichokes to the heart, such as for the Asparagus, Artichoke & Chickpea Ragout (page 49).

Outer leaves from 2 large artichokes (see Prep Tip, page 122)

1½ **to 2 tablespoons olive oil**

Kosher salt

Herb-Citrus Butter (page 100), melted and kept warm, or mayonnaise for dipping

The leaves left over from paring an artichoke down to the heart have a little bit of edible artichoke heart still attached, and you can eat them just like you would a whole steamed artichoke, by dipping the leaves in mayonnaise or melted butter and then scraping the little bit of goodness off with your teeth. With this recipe, you first steam the leaves to cook them through, then you quickly roast them to add crispiness and extra flavor from caramelization in the hot oven. If you run out of time, you can serve them straightaway after steaming.

....

Preheat the oven to 425°F.

Place the artichoke leaves in a large steamer and steam until the edible part on the inside edge of the leaves is tender, 15 to 20 minutes, stirring occasionally. Remove the leaves from the steamer. If you like, you can serve them at this point.

Otherwise, spread the leaves on a large baking sheet. Drizzle the olive oil on top, sprinkle with salt to taste, then toss the leaves to coat. Spread the leaves out in a single layer and roast until slightly browned, 7 to 10 minutes. Check the leaves at 7 minutes; don't leave them in the oven too long as they can get tough and shrink.

Serve immediately with the Herb-Citrus Butter or mayonnaise alongside.

Squash Blossoms

For me, squash blossoms are always an impulse buy. Because I'm never sure when they'll be around, I don't usually plan on them for a menu, but when I see them at the farmers' market—usually the best source for these highly perishable items aside from a vegetable garden—I find them difficult to resist. From that point of view, squash blossoms aren't something you're likely to have leftover from other cooking projects, unless you happen to have just harvested a bunch of baby zucchini with the flowers attached. But they are a delicious part of a popular plant that we don't always think to cook.

The male flowers of a zucchini or other squash plant, the blossoms are a few inches long, with meaty, edible stems that you can use as handles when cooking and eating the whole flowers.

In the United States, the squash blossoms sold in markets are usually zucchini blossoms, but winter squash blossoms are also used in other parts of the world. In Mexico, where they're called *flor de calabaza*, cooks sauté them and stuff them into quesadillas and add them to soups. In Italy, the *fiori di zucca* or *fiori di zucchini* are often breaded and fried or added to a frittata, two of my favorite uses for them.

Keep squash blossoms dry when you store them in the refrigerator, and use within a day.

FONTINA-STUFFED SQUASH BLOSSOM FRITTERS SERVES 4

12 to 15 zucchini blossoms, with the stem on

⅓ cup shredded fontina cheese

⅓ cup crumbled fresh goat cheese

Pinch of dried or fresh rosemary, thyme, or oregano

Freshly ground pepper

Batter

½ cup cornmeal

½ cup all-purpose flour

½ teaspoon kosher salt

Freshly ground pepper

2 large eggs

½ cup milk

Vegetable oil, for frying

Kosher salt, to serve

Though you can just slice and sauté squash blossoms, I usually like to keep them whole, especially since the flowers are just big enough to hold a pocket of cheese. A mix of a melty fontina with tangy fresh goat cheese is lovely, but you can also just tuck small cubes of Gruyère, mozzarella, or Monterey Jack inside each flower. The cornmeal batter helps hold everything together as you pan-fry the flowers, though don't be concerned if a little bit of cheese melts out and mingles with the crispy coating. It just adds to their deliciousness and charm.

....

Remove the bright yellow stamen from inside each blossom by gently opening up the petals and snapping off the stamen at the base. Do your best not to tear the petals. Leave the stems on the flowers.

In a small bowl, combine the fontina, goat cheese, thyme, and pepper to taste. Roll the cheese mixture into balls ½ to 1 teaspoon in size, depending on the size of the blossoms. Stuff a cheese ball into each blossom and gently close the petals around it.

To make the batter, in a shallow bowl, combine the cornmeal, flour, salt, and pepper to taste. In another bowl, beat together the eggs and milk. Place the batter ingredients and prepared flowers next to the stove.

Place a large frying pan over medium heat and add enough vegetable oil to fill by ¼ to ½ inch. Line a platter with paper towels.

→

When the oil is hot enough to sizzle when you add a drop of batter, hold a flower by the stem and dip it first into the egg mixture and then into the cornmeal mixture, allowing excess to drip off, then gently add it to the oil. Cook 6 to 8 flowers at a time, without crowding, until lightly browned and crisp, 4 to 5 minutes per side. Remove from the oil with a slotted spoon and drain on the paper towels. Repeat with the remaining flowers. Sprinkle with salt and serve immediately.

Broccoli

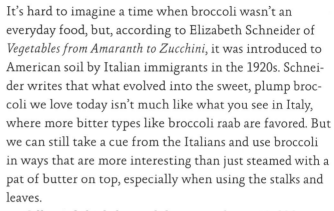

It's hard to imagine a time when broccoli wasn't an everyday food, but, according to Elizabeth Schneider of *Vegetables from Amaranth to Zucchini*, it was introduced to American soil by Italian immigrants in the 1920s. Schneider writes that what evolved into the sweet, plump broccoli we love today isn't much like what you see in Italy, where more bitter types like broccoli raab are favored. But we can still take a cue from the Italians and use broccoli in ways that are more interesting than just steamed with a pat of butter on top, especially when using the stalks and leaves.

Silky and thick, broccoli leaves can be sautéed like any braising green, though you're most likely to encounter large quantities of them when you grow the vegetable yourself. With the exception of the thick, fibrous outer layer, broccoli stalks are perfectly edible. In fact, I think they're the sweetest part of the vegetable. Some people recommend using a vegetable peeler to peel them, but I find it easier to use a chef's knife. You're left with long, rectangular batons of crunchy, sweet broccoli, which are delicious raw in a Shaved Broccoli Stalk Salad with Lime & Cotija (page 129), seared to make Golden Broccoli Spears with Tangerine Peel (page 130), or chopped and simmered in Broccoli Stalk Orecchiette with Anchovies & Garlic Bread Crumbs (page 131).

Broccoli is at its sweetest the sooner you eat it, but if you wrap and refrigerate it, it will hold for 3 to 4 days.

Prep Tip

To make broccoli batons, first remove the stalks at the base of the florets, then trim the tough ends. Cut the stalks into batons by removing the thick, tough outer layer, using four long cuts with a chef's knife.

SHAVED BROCCOLI STALK SALAD WITH LIME & COTIJA SERVES 2

Leaves and stalks from 1 bunch broccoli (about 3 stalks), cut into batons (see Prep Tip, page 127)

1 tablespoon extra-virgin olive oil

1½ teaspoons fresh lime juice

Kosher salt and freshly ground pepper

¼ cup crumbled cotija or feta cheese

While waiting for a main course to finish cooking, you can make this simple salad with the remnants of a bunch of broccoli. Or, you can integrate the shaved broccoli, which is sweet, mild, and tender, into other lettuce-based salads, or julienne the strips for cabbage slaws, such as the Celery Slaw with Apple Peel & Ginger Dressing (page 52).

Place the broccoli batons flat on a cutting board, then use a sharp vegetable peeler to shave the broccoli into paper-thin strips.

Place the shaved broccoli and leaves in a medium bowl and toss with the olive oil, lime juice, and salt and pepper to taste. Gently fold in the cheese and serve immediately.

GOLDEN BROCCOLI SPEARS
WITH TANGERINE PEEL SERVES 1 TO 2

Peanut oil

Pinch of red chile flakes

Leaves and stalks from
1 bunch broccoli (about
3 stalks), cut into batons
(see Prep Tip, page 127)

Kosher salt

½ teaspoon tangerine
zest, finely grated with
a Microplane or cut into
thin strips with a knife or
zester

Splash of sherry vinegar

Sear broccoli spears and their tender leaves in a cast-iron pan for a side dish or quick cook's snack. You can also chop the seared broccoli and add it to fried rice or Chinese noodle dishes.

Heat enough peanut oil to lightly coat the bottom of a cast-iron or other heavy pan over medium heat. Add the red chile flakes, swirl to coat the pan, then add the broccoli pieces and leaves and sprinkle with salt.

Sear until the broccoli is singed, golden, and cooked through, 2 to 3 minutes per side.

Stir in the tangerine peel and sherry vinegar, being careful to avoid splattering when adding it to the hot oil, and toss to coat for 30 seconds. Adjust seasoning and serve immediately.

BROCCOLI STALK ORECCHIETTE WITH ANCHOVIES & GARLIC BREAD CRUMBS SERVES 2 TO 3

3 cups (8 ounces) broccoli batons (see Prep Tip, page 127), leaves, and florets, cut into 1-inch pieces

8 ounces orecchiette pasta

4 tablespoons extra-virgin olive oil, plus more for drizzling

4 cloves garlic, minced

1 cup fresh bread crumbs, or ½ cup dry bread crumbs or panko

¼ teaspoon red chile flakes, plus more to taste

4 to 6 anchovy fillets

Kosher salt

If you eat a lot of broccoli, you can save up the leftover stalks for use in this savory pasta, or use a combination of stalks and florets, which is also a good option if you'd like to double the recipe. Cauliflower works well here too, and chopped black olives, capers, and preserved lemon all make great additions— or substitutions for the anchovies if you want to make a vegetarian version.

. . . .

Bring a large pot of well-salted water to boil.

Blanch the broccoli batons, leaves, and florets in the boiling water until crisp-tender, about 3 minutes. Remove with a slotted spoon or skimmer to a plate, then add the pasta to the water and cook to al dente according to the package directions. When done, drain the pasta, reserving 1 cup of the pasta water.

Meanwhile, heat 2 tablespoons of the olive oil in a large frying pan over medium heat. Add half of the garlic. When it smells garlicky, after about 30 seconds, add the bread crumbs. Sauté without stirring until the crumbs are browned on the bottom, then stir occasionally until browned and crisp all over, 3 to 5 minutes total. Remove from the pan and set aside.

Add the remaining 2 tablespoons of olive oil, the remaining garlic, and the red chile flakes to the pan. When the garlic is fragrant, add the drained broccoli and cook, stirring, until integrated with the sauce, about 2 minutes. Make room in the center of the pan for the anchovies,

→

then add them and crush to form a paste, cooking only about 30 seconds to preserve their flavor.

Add the pasta to the pan and stir in enough of the pasta cooking water to form a sauce, then stir over low heat for 2 to 3 minutes. Season with salt and more red chile flakes to taste. Stir in the toasted bread crumbs and serve immediately in pasta bowls with a drizzle of olive oil.

Cauliflower

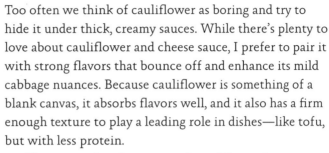

Too often we think of cauliflower as boring and try to hide it under thick, creamy sauces. While there's plenty to love about cauliflower and cheese sauce, I prefer to pair it with strong flavors that bounce off and enhance its mild cabbage nuances. Because cauliflower is something of a blank canvas, it absorbs flavors well, and it also has a firm enough texture to play a leading role in dishes—like tofu, but with less protein.

The conventional way to cook cauliflower is to remove the florets from the less tender stalk at the core. But that means losing a fairly large and completely edible chunk of the vegetable, including the edible leaves that are often attached, which have a flavor similar to cabbage, but less pronounced. The stalk actually has a satisfyingly dense texture, and to take advantage of this quality, you can cut clear through the head to create steaklike cauliflower pieces. Note that smaller cauliflower or heads with thinner stems don't hold together as well, since the stem connects the florets, but even if the slices crumble into smaller pieces, they will still work in the following recipes.

To store cauliflower, place it in a plastic bag and refrigerate it. It will keep for 5 days.

Prep Tip

To prepare cauliflower steaks and leaves, first remove the outer leaves from the cauliflower and trim the very bottom of the stalk. Place upright and use a large knife to cut through the florets and stalk, making ½-inch-thick slices. (In addition to the steaks, you will have some smaller pieces that aren't connected to the core.) If the leaves are large, remove the ribs and cook them separately, and longer, than the leaves.

PAN-ROASTED CAULIFLOWER STEAKS WITH TOMATOES & CAPERS SERVES 2

2 tablespoons olive oil

2 cloves garlic, thinly sliced

¼ teaspoon red chile flakes

½ head cauliflower, cut into steaks (see Prep Tip, page 133), plus any leaves

Kosher salt

1 cup cherry tomatoes, halved

2 tablespoons capers (soaked in water if salted), drained

1 tablespoon chopped Italian parsley (optional)

Cauliflower "steaks"—cauliflower cut crosswise into ½-inch pieces—brown well in olive oil. A scattering of cherry tomatoes, capers, garlic, and red chile flakes adds a southern Italian flavor that belies cauliflower's usual bland identity. The leaves, which you're more likely to get from cauliflower purchased at the farmers' market, are particularly delicious in this dish. If your cauliflower doesn't have any leaves, Italian parsley can add some green to the plate.

Heat the olive oil in a large cast-iron frying pan over medium heat. Add the garlic and red chile flakes and swirl until fragrant. Add the cauliflower steaks, which should fit in the pan in a single layer, and any extra cauliflower pieces, making sure they are all touching the pan. Season to taste with salt.

Cook the steaks without turning until caramelized, about 8 minutes, then flip and cook until browned on the bottom and tender, another 8 to 10 minutes. During the last few minutes, add the cauliflower leaves, tomatoes, and capers and cook until the tomatoes and leaves wilt.

Adjust the seasoning with salt, scatter with parsley, and serve immediately.

CAULIFLOWER WITH SMOKED PAPRIKA & WHOLE WHEAT LINGUINE SERVES 6

1 pound whole wheat linguine or spaghetti

½ head cauliflower and leaves

¼ cup extra-virgin olive oil

½ cup finely chopped red onion

1 tablespoon chopped garlic

2 teaspoons chopped fresh oregano, thyme, or a combination

2 teaspoons smoked paprika, or to taste

Kosher salt

2 cups canned tomato puree

½ cup shredded mozzarella or fontina cheese

¼ cup chopped Italian parsley

Grated Pecorino cheese, to serve

For this recipe, you use cauliflower florets, as well as the core and leaves, in a light tomato-based pasta sauce served over whole wheat linguine. Smoked paprika intensifies the sweetness of the tomatoes, and its low-voltage spice is matched by the cauliflower's slight cabbage-y flavor. Adding just a little mozzarella to the sauce helps it cling better to the pasta. You could also use fontina, Monterey Jack, or any other odds and ends of creamy, meltable cheese you have on hand.

Note: Smoked paprika, or pimentón, is available at specialty stores. You can substitute sweet paprika.

Bring a large pot of salted water to a boil for the pasta, then cook according to the package directions. Drain, reserving 1 cup of the cooking water.

Meanwhile, slice the cauliflower through the core into ¼-inch slices, then ¼-inch mini florets and cubes. Reserve any leaves; if very large, chop into 1-inch pieces.

Heat the olive oil in a large sauté pan over medium-low heat. Add the onion, garlic, and oregano and sauté until the onion is translucent, about 3 minutes. Add the smoked paprika and sauté a few minutes more. If the mixture gets too brown, add a few tablespoons of the pasta water. Stir in the cauliflower and leaves and season with salt to taste. Toss to coat in the oil and sauté until lightly browned, 3 minutes. Add the tomato puree, bring to a simmer, cover, and cook until the cauliflower is tender, about 5 minutes. Season to taste with salt.

To serve, stir the mozzarella and parsley into the sauce. Place the linguine back in the pot or a warmed serving bowl and toss in the sauce with enough of the reserved pasta water to coat the pasta. Serve immediately in shallow bowls with the Pecorino alongside.

BROILED CAULIFLOWER STEAKS WITH MUSTARD GLAZE SERVES 4

1 head cauliflower, 1½ to 2 pounds, cut into steaks (see Prep Tip, page 133)

2 tablespoons whole-grain Dijon mustard

2 tablespoons olive oil

1 tablespoon soy sauce

1 teaspoon honey

1 to 2 tablespoons water

Kosher salt and freshly ground pepper

As you often see in Indian cooking, cauliflower pairs beautifully with bold spices. In this recipe, you slather cauliflower with a mustard-based glaze that contains soy sauce, olive oil, and honey for added finesse. It comes out from under the broiler tender and crispy, making a succulent side dish for roasted meats. The steaks are also delicious prepared on the grill, but the smaller ends of the cauliflower will fall through the grate, which is why broiling is better here.

Note: Broiled cauliflower makes a fantastic filling for panini. Spread some of the glaze that collects in the pan on ciabatta bread before stuffing it with the cauliflower, slices of Gouda or Gruyère cheese, and watercress or arugula, then toast the sandwiches in a panini press or in a lightly oiled cast-iron pan.

Arrange an oven rack 6 inches from the heating element and preheat the broiler.

Spread the cauliflower pieces in a 13 by 9-inch or larger baking dish to fit in a single layer.

Combine the mustard, olive oil, soy sauce, and honey in a small bowl. Whisk in 1 or 2 tablespoons of water to thin the glaze, then drizzle over the cauliflower and brush to coat the top evenly. Let marinate at room temperature for 10 to 30 minutes.

Season the cauliflower lightly with salt and pepper. Broil until golden and mostly tender, 10 minutes (watch carefully to prevent burning), then flip the cauliflower over and cook until tender, another 5 minutes. Serve warm or at room temperature.

SEEDS

Seeds are the part of a plant that grows after it has flow-ered, and the edible kinds are among some of our most common foods, such as corn and peas. In this country, we tend to think of these foods in their fresh forms, yet many cultures see them more as grains that are dried and ground into flour, such as fava flour used to make falafel in the Middle East and cornmeal, traditionally used for breads and cereals in the Americas. Seeds tend to come in complicated wrappers—fava beans must be shelled first, then peeled; corn has to be shucked, then removed from the cob. These husks and shells capture a lot of the flavor of the vegetable, and to make the most of these foods, we could use these resources more often in the kitchen.

Season: Peas are a springtime vegetable, favas are around in spring and early summer, and corn arrives in summer.

Smoky Corn Cob Chowder 145

Corn-Pancetta Puddings in
Corn Husk Baskets 147

Whole Grilled Favas 151

Pea Pod Pudding 153

Corn

With its husks, silk, and cobs, corn is an obvious candidate for the whole vegetable treatment. While dried corn husks are common in Mexican cooking, fresh ones are usually thrown out. Still, they can be used in creative ways, such as to make baskets for sides like the Corn-Pancetta Puddings (page 147). After you remove the kernels, corn cobs are full of juicy flavor that you can scrape out to use in the pudding, or coax into a broth for a Smoky Corn Cob Chowder (page 145).

Corn on the cob can hold for 2 to 3 days in the refrigerator, wrapped in plastic bags. Store extra corn husks for later use in zip-top bags in the refrigerator for 2 to 3 days.

Prep Tip

To remove the kernels from an ear of corn, hold upright on a cutting board and cut off the kernels with a sharp knife.

SMOKY CORN COB CHOWDER SERVES 6

Use the potato skins and bacon fat in the Potato Skin–Bacon Fat Chips (page 38).

3 ears of corn, husked

1 poblano chile

3 slices bacon, diced small (optional)

1 tablespoon unsalted butter

1 cup diced onion

2 cloves garlic, minced

1 quart Vegetable Scraps Stock (page 10) or low-sodium chicken or vegetable broth

2 russet potatoes, peeled and diced small

Kosher salt

¾ cup heavy cream

Freshly ground pepper

This classic creamy soup gets extra complexity from roasted poblano chiles, which have the grassy quality and tender texture of bell peppers with a deeper, spicy note. Roasting the peppers and corn over a gas burner or grill adds more smoky flavor to balance the sweetness of the broth.

Roast the corn and poblano on a grill over low heat (around 300°F), or place directly over gas burners, until the corn takes on a smoky hue and the poblano is blackened on all sides, turning often, 10 to 12 minutes. Place the poblano in a plastic bag and let steam for 10 minutes, then peel off the blackened skin, remove the seeds, and dice. Cut the kernels from the cobs, reserving the cobs.

Fry the bacon in a large, heavy stockpot or Dutch oven over medium heat until almost crunchy, about 5 minutes. Drain off most of the bacon grease, leaving the bacon in the pan. Melt the butter in the pot, then add the onion and sauté until translucent, 7 to 10 minutes. Add the garlic and cook until fragrant, about 30 seconds.

Add the broth. Scrape the reserved corn cobs into the pot to remove all the milk, then add the cobs to the pot with half of the potato. Bring to a boil, cover, and season with salt and pepper. Reduce the heat to a simmer and cook until the potato pieces are very soft, 20 to 25 minutes. Remove the corn cobs and mash the potatoes with a potato masher. Add the remaining potatoes, corn kernels, poblanos, and salt to taste and cook until the potatoes are tender, 12 to 15 minutes.

Add the cream and simmer gently for about 5 minutes. Adjust the seasoning and serve immediately.

CORN-PANCETTA PUDDINGS IN CORN HUSK BASKETS MAKES 18 SMALL PUDDINGS; SERVES 6 TO 9

Use any extra corn kernels (the amount you will get from two ears of corn varies) in the Radish Leaf Salad with Corn, Tomatoes & Salted Cucumbers (page 29).

2 ears of corn

¾ cup heavy cream

¾ cup milk

3 ounces pancetta, diced small

4 large eggs

¼ cup unsalted butter or a mixture of butter and rendered pancetta fat, melted and cooled

½ cup all-purpose flour

½ cup polenta or cornmeal

1 tablespoon sugar

1 teaspoon baking powder

¾ teaspoon kosher salt

Pinch of freshly ground pepper

Pinch of cayenne

½ cup seeded and diced tomatoes

These savory puddings work as a brunch or side dish, with their corn husk "handles" making them look like cheerful sunflowers. After you remove the kernels from the cobs, you scrape the corn milk from the cobs with the back of a knife, then simmer the cobs in cream and milk. This mixture forms the base of the pudding batter, which you pour into corn husk–lined muffin tins. The result is part corn muffin, part soufflé.

Preheat the oven to 350°F. Grease a 12-cup muffin tin plus 6 cups of an additional tin.

Bring a large pot of water to a boil. Trim the leafy tops of the husks from each ear of corn and slice through the bottom of the cob to more easily remove the husks. Discarding the tougher outer husks, trim off any extra curved part of the more tender inner husks, and tear the husks in half lengthwise until you have 36 strips about the width of your muffin tins. Blanch in the water until softened, 5 minutes. Drain and let cool.

Holding the cobs upright on a cutting board, cut the kernels off the cobs, then measure out 1 cup; reserve any extra kernels for another use. Place the cream and milk in a small saucepan, and use the back of a knife to scrape any remaining corn and juices from the cobs into the pan. Place the cobs in the pan (break them in half to fit), bring to a simmer, and simmer gently for 15 minutes. Allow to cool in the pan.

Place the pancetta in a small sauté pan over medium heat and brown until crisp, about 6 minutes. Drain on paper towels (save the remaining fat to replace of some of the butter, if you like).

Before mixing the batter, press a strip of corn husk into a muffin tin, and top with a thinner strip to make a cross pattern with the ends sticking up. Repeat to use the remaining husks (if the husks pop out of place, just poke them down again) until you have lined 18 cups.

Remove the cobs from the cooled cream mixture and place the mixture in a large bowl with the eggs, butter, flour, polenta, sugar, baking powder, salt, pepper, and cayenne. Fold in the 1 cup corn kernels, tomatoes, and half of the pancetta, then pour into the prepared baskets. Top with the remaining pancetta and bake until firm, about 20 minutes. Use a narrow silicone spatula or dinner knife to remove the puddings from the pan and serve immediately, or slightly warm.

Fava Beans

With a unique nutty flavor and intensely green color, fresh fava beans are a harbinger of spring, but they can be a high-maintenance vegetable. Each pound of whole pods results in only 1 cup of beans, and they traditionally require two rounds of peeling: you first remove the beans from their fuzzy pods, then blanch them and remove the inner skins. I usually recruit my children to help with the two peeling stages. But when we can't deal with all that, I've learned to grill them whole (page 151). The outer pods become soft enough to eat, and the beans inside are steamed through and tender, ready to eat out of hand.

Keep whole fava beans wrapped in plastic bags for up to 1 week in the refrigerator.

WHOLE GRILLED FAVAS SERVES 2 TO 4

1 pound fava beans in
the pod

1 tablespoon olive oil

½ teaspoon kosher salt

If you grill whole favas until the beans steam inside, you can serve them whole and let everyone do the work at the table. Smaller or younger favas, especially, become completely edible when grilled, though the pods have strings and a slightly bitter flavor that not everyone will love. While some will want to munch on the whole shebang, others may opt to remove the beans from the pods, like edamame, and then squeeze the beans out of their inner cases before eating them. Either way, it's an interactive and delicious bar snack around the grill.

Preheat a grill to medium-low heat (300° to 350°F).

In a large bowl, toss the fava beans with the olive oil and salt.

Place the favas on the grill perpendicular to the grates (as pictured on page 149) so they don't fall through, and grill until marked and puffed up, about 15 minutes, turning once or twice. Open a pod and taste a fava bean; it should be just about cooked through. Remove from the grill and let steam in the pods for a few minutes before serving.

Eat the whole pods (except the strings), if tender enough, or peel and eat just the individual beans.

Peas

Fresh English peas are not cheap, and it seems a shame to throw out all those bright green, crunchy pods. If you bite into one, you'll notice they're very juicy and sweet but too stringy to eat. While they always work in stock for a springtime soup, you can also use pea pods in a savory custard that tastes surprisingly just like the peas themselves (page 153). And if you ever see pea shoots or pea sprouts—the tender shoots and leaves from a snow pea plant—at the farmers' market or an Asian grocer, be sure to grab them for a stir-fry. Just remove any tougher stems and stir-fry them with chopped garlic as in the Garlic-Braised Greens (page 87), adding some sliced ginger with the garlic and omitting the lemon. Like pea pods, they capture that fresh essence-of-pea flavor you can only enjoy in spring.

Keep peas or their pods wrapped in a plastic bag for 1 to 2 days in the refrigerator.

PEA POD PUDDING SERVES 4 TO 6

2 cups heavy cream

1 teaspoon sugar

1 teaspoon kosher salt

Pods from 1 pound
English peas

3 large eggs

Freshly ground pepper

One of the first recipes I had to test as a culinary school intern at the *San Francisco Chronicle* was a duck liver flan from Bay Wolf restaurant in Oakland. Not accustomed to savory pudding, I honestly thought it sounded pretty disgusting at the time. Yet it was incredible, with the rich liver set off by green peppercorns and cream, and it changed my mind about savory flan forever. So when I had a pile of sweet, crisp English pea pods left over from cooking fresh peas, I infused cream with the pods and then made a flan that had a subtle yet definitive pea flavor. Its delicate texture makes it a shoo-in to accompany fish or lamb, while larger servings make a stunning first course.

Note: The peas themselves are not used in this recipe. Serve them on the side or another time, but don't wait too long to use either the peas or pods, as their sweetness will fade.

Preheat the oven to 325°F. Place six 4-ounce or four 6-ounce ramekins inside a 13 by 9-inch baking dish. (The smaller ones are perfect as a side dish, while the larger ones are better for a first course.)

Place the cream, sugar, and salt in a medium saucepan over medium-low heat. Stir to dissolve the sugar and salt, then add the pea pods. Bring the cream to the barest of simmers, stirring occasionally; the pods will shrink down as they soften. Reduce the heat to low, cover, and steam for 10 minutes. Remove from the heat and let steep, covered, for 20 minutes.

Bring a kettle of water to a boil.

➡

With a fine-mesh strainer, strain the cream mixture into a large liquid measuring cup or other pouring pitcher. In a large bowl, whisk the eggs and pepper to taste together until very smooth. Whisking constantly, slowly pour some of the cream mixture into the eggs (this will temper the eggs and keep them from cooking from the heat of the cream). Once you have added about a quarter of the cream mixture, you can add the rest of it more quickly. Whisk until very smooth, then strain the mixture back into the measuring cup. Pour the custard into the ramekins, then pour hot or boiling water around the ramekins so that it reaches 1 inch up the sides of the dish. Cover the pan with foil and bake until the puddings are set, 30 minutes.

Serve the puddings hot or warm in the ramekins.

FRUIT

Though this book is mainly about vegetables, it's impossible to talk about stems, seeds, and flowers without diving into fruit, too. First of all, I couldn't ignore all those important fruits that we eat as vegetables, such as tomatoes, squash, and avocados. And then there are a few everyday fruit-fruits, such as apples and melons, that have so many valuable extra parts that it would be a shame not to mention them as well. As a cook, it helps to think about what fruits have in common, namely seeds, since fruit is the way a plant spreads its progeny. Some, like avocado seeds, have little culinary use, while others are plenty useful, such as winter squash seeds that you can toast and sprinkle over soup, or clusters of tomato seeds holding delicious tomato water.

Season: Most fruit is available from spring to fall, starting with avocados, strawberries, and cherries, then moving on to other stone fruits, cucumber, tomatoes, melons, and apples, and finally winter squash and citrus.

Extra-Fruit Crisp **161**

Apple-Wine "Jus" & Jelly **163**

Apple Peel Bourbon **164**

Avocado Lassi **169**

Avocado-Lemon Dressing with Toasted Cumin **170**

Harissa-Roasted Squash with Warm Chickpea & Mâche Salad **172**

Butternut Squash Soup with Toasted Seeds **174**

Dried Citrus Zest **177**

Crispy Lemon Cookies **178**

Fresh Tomato Paste in Olive Oil **181**

Tomato Water–Cucumber Granita **183**

Thai Watermelon Salad with Crunchy Watermelon Rind **187**

Fruit & Herbal Syrups, Chunky & Clear **189**

Watermelon Agua Fresca **191**

Lemony Watermelon Rind Pickles **192**

Apples

When you core and peel apples for an apple pie or tart, there is always a heap of peels and cores left over, all packed with flavor and pectin, the natural thickening agent that makes jams thick. Simmer the cores with some wine, sugar, and water and you have a reduction that tastes like a grown up version of apple juice (page 163). Keep cooking it and it will eventually turn to jelly. Apples have more pectin than other fruits, so you can wrap apple cores and skin in cheesecloth—or just a few apple wedges—and add it to the pot when you are making other jams, like blackberry, for natural thickening. But the easiest way to use up apple cores and skins, it must be said, is to infuse them into bourbon or other types of alcohol for making fall drinks (see page 164).

Any type of apple works great in the following recipes, but the Apple Wine Jus (and jelly, if you make it; page 163) will be a pretty shade of pink if you use red varieties.

Apples refrigerate well, stored in a plastic bag, for 2 weeks.

EXTRA-FRUIT CRISP SERVES 8

If using peeled apples, use the peels in the Apple-Wine "Jus" & Jelly (page 163) or Apple Peel Bourbon (page 164).

Fruit filling

- 6 cups fruit, cored, pitted, or hulled and cut in ½-inch dice, smaller berries left whole (see Note)
- ¼ cup sugar
- 2 tablespoons unsalted butter, melted
- 1 tablespoon all-purpose flour
- 1 tablespoon fresh lemon juice
- ⅛ teaspoon kosher salt
- ½ teaspoon cinnamon and ¼ teaspoon allspice (optional; good for apples)
- ½ teaspoon ground cardamom (optional; good for plums)

Crumble

- ½ cup cold unsalted butter, cubed
- ½ cup all-purpose flour
- ¼ cup light brown sugar
- ½ teaspoon cinnamon
- ¼ teaspoon kosher salt
- ½ cup rolled oats
- ½ cup finely chopped walnuts (optional)

When you have too much fruit and would like to turn it into a dessert, making a fruit crisp is much easier than assembling a pie. All you need to do is chop up the fruit—peeling it isn't necessary—and toss it with sugar, lemon juice, and spices. Then spread the mixture out in a baking dish, top it with a quick crumble, and bake until bubbly and jammy. Below are various options for using up different types of fruit, depending on what you have around. Rather than using all berries, I like to use a mix of berries and stone fruit.

Note: To get 6 cups of fruit, you can use 2 pounds apples (peeled or unpeeled); 3 pounds stone fruit, such as plums, apricots, peaches, or cherries; or 2¼ pounds blackberries, blueberries, raspberries, or strawberries. If you don't have 6 cups of fruit, reduce the amount of filling ingredients proportionately to the amount of fruit you have, pour the filling into as many ramekins as it will fill, and then top each ramekin with 3 or 4 tablespoons of the crumble mixture.

Preheat the oven to 350°F.

To make the fruit filling, combine all of the filling ingredients in a large bowl.

To make the crumble, in a large bowl combine the butter, flour, brown sugar, cinnamon, and salt. Use a pastry cutter or two forks to mix together until the butter is in small chunks. Stir in the oats and the walnuts. (The crumble will hold, tightly covered, in the freezer for 1 month.)

➡

Pack the fruit filling into an 8 by 8-inch baking dish, a medium gratin dish, or 8 to 10 ramekins, then spread the crumble evenly on top. Bake until the fruit is tender and bubbly and the topping looks solid and is no longer shiny, 45 minutes to 1 hour for apples, 30 to 40 minutes for stone fruit or berries. Let cool on a rack for 20 minutes, then serve warm.

APPLE-WINE "JUS" & JELLY

MAKES 3 TO 4 CUPS; ENOUGH FOR 6 TO 8 DRINKS

Peels and cores from 2 pounds or 6 to 8 apples (4 cups loosely packed scraps)

6 cups water

1 cup dry white wine, such as Pinot Grigio

¾ cup sugar

Sprigs of thyme, strips of lemon rind, or thin slices of fresh ginger (optional)

This sweet broth is made by simmering the apple cores and peels left over from making a pie to create a base for beverages. To make a version of what's called Apfelschorle in Germany, use 1 part jus and 2 parts sparkling water or club soda. Or, add a splash of booze–gin, brandy, bourbon, or Calvados–and you have an easy fall cocktail to launch a meal that will end, happily, in apple pie. Because the juice contains so much natural pectin, I offer the option of continuing to cook it into an apple-wine jelly, which is yummy on toast or can be melted to top classic fruit tarts.

Place all of the ingredients in a medium saucepan. Bring to a simmer and cook over medium-low heat until the liquid is very thick and has reduced by about half, 45 minutes. Strain through a fine-mesh strainer, pressing the solids to extract as much liquid as possible.

Chill before serving with sparkling water. Or, for a cocktail, pour 1 part jus and 1 part alcohol over ice. Float with club soda and garnish with a lemon wedge.

To make apple-wine jelly, place the strained apple-wine "jus" in a small saucepan. Continue simmering until the liquid is reduced to ¾ cup or 1 cup and has reached the jell state, another 30 to 45 minutes. To test it, place a small plate in the freezer during cooking, then add a drop of jelly to the cold plate and return it to the freezer for a few minutes. If it is thick and looks like jelly, it's done. If not, continue cooking until it reaches that state. Pour the jelly into a clean half-pint jar and let cool. The jelly can be stored, refrigerated, for up to 1 month.

APPLE PEEL BOURBON MAKES 750 ML

Infusing fruit and herbs into alcohol is a time-honored tradition, but using scraps instead of whole fruit may be a modern-day variation. Instead of bourbon, try brandy, whisky, rum, or vodka; really, anything that sounds like it would be delicious with apples probably is. Then drink the spirit neat—the apple softens its rough edges—or use in cocktails.

For a take on a classic cocktail, pour a shot of Apple Peel Bourbon over ice. Top with ginger ale or ginger beer and a generous squeeze of lime (as pictured on page 167).

Note: You can also use apple cores, though the seeds impart a slight hint of their distinctive tannic flavor into the alcohol.

Peels from 1½ to
2 pounds apples

4 whole cloves

1 cinnamon stick

1 750-ml bottle bourbon

Place the bourbon in a nonreactive container, such as a half-gallon jar, and add the cloves, cinnamon stick, and just enough apple peels to fill the jar without any of the peels being exposed to the air. Shake the jar.

Let the apple peels infuse into the alcohol at room temperature, shaking the contents of the jar often, until the flavor is pronounced, about 1 week. If you'd like a lighter cinnamon flavor, remove the cinnamon after 1 to 2 days, tasting it first. Strain through a fine-mesh strainer and keep in an airtight container, refrigerated, for several months.

Avocados

Avocados don't have extra parts that are routinely wasted. Instead, it's the fruit itself that doesn't get put to full use. The problem with a ripe avocado—a beautiful, creamy, dreamlike, ripe avocado—is that there's no gray area. It can take a while to ripen, but when it's ripe, it's ripe. You can put it in the refrigerator to slow down its decline, but only for a day or so. Then, if you use half an avocado in a sandwich or salad, there's that other half that will turn brown on you.

Of course, there are lots of tricks for keeping half an avocado from browning, including rubbing it with lemon juice or leaving in the pit. Even better, add it to an acidic sauce, such as the Cilantro Salsa (page 108) or the Avocado-Lemon Dressing with Toasted Cumin (page 170) to keep it green and fresh for days. I also love what one friend showed me how to do, which is to make a lassi (page 169), which is essentially an avocado smoothie. It adds a whole new perspective on avocados, celebrating their sweet and fruity side in a spontaneous, taking-full-advantage-of-the-avocados-in-your-life kind of way.

Keep avocados at room temperature until ripe, then refrigerate for up to 1 day to slow ripening.

AVOCADO LASSI MAKES 1 SMALL DRINK

½ ripe avocado

½ cup milk

2 tablespoons plain yogurt

½ teaspoon sugar, or more to taste

Pinch of kosher salt

Ice (optional)

When you have that half an avocado left over, don't throw it out. Blend it into this not-too-sweet energizing drink, which was introduced to me by my friend Amanda Berne, a colleague at the *San Francisco Chronicle*. Though traditional lassis contain more yogurt, its tanginess can overpower the subtle flavor of the avocado. And, because our palates are all attuned to the savory side of avocado, as in guacamole, it's tempting to add lemon juice, but that takes away from avocado's mild, tropical fruitiness, which is celebrated here.

If you have an immersion blender (and you aren't using ice), scoop the avocado into a tall, narrow glass and add the remaining ingredients. Process to blend, adding more sugar if you like. If you'd like to make it with ice, combine all of the ingredients and a handful of ice in a regular blender and puree until smooth. Pour into an 8-ounce glass and serve immediately.

AVOCADO-LEMON DRESSING WITH TOASTED CUMIN MAKES 1 CUP

½ teaspoon cumin seeds

1 ripe avocado

¼ cup extra-virgin olive oil

2 tablespoons fresh lemon juice, plus more as needed

2 tablespoons plain yogurt, plus more as needed

¾ teaspoon kosher salt

Freshly ground pepper

1 shallot, finely chopped

2 to 4 tablespoons water

If you have a delicious avocado that is in danger of going bad, turn it into this salad dressing that will last for several days in the refrigerator. The acidity of the lemon and the yogurt in this dressing keeps the avocado surprisingly fresh and bright green. You can easily halve this recipe if you have only half an avocado. Note that this dressing is on the thick side; if you add less water, it can double as a dip.

Note: This would also be a good place for any extra cilantro that needs using up. Chop up a few tablespoons and add it to taste.

Place the cumin seeds in a small sauté pan over medium-low heat. Toast until fragrant, watching carefully to keep them from burning, 4 to 5 minutes. Let cool, then grind in a spice grinder or crush with a mortar and pestle.

Place the avocado in a medium bowl and mash with a fork, then work in the olive oil, lemon juice, yogurt, salt, pepper to taste, and cumin. Stir in the shallot and then add enough water to thin to a pouring consistency for a salad dressing. Or, thin it with additional yogurt or lemon juice.

The dressing will keep, covered tightly, for 3 days in the refrigerator.

Butternut Squash

I always think of butternut and other types of winter squash as food within a fortress. It's a good thing these hard squashes hold so long, because the thought of cracking into one can be a disincentive to cooking it. It requires a large, sharp knife, a steady cutting board, and some muscle. But once you've split one in half, it is not so challenging to cook. Just scoop out the seeds and stick them on a pan to roast until tender, then scrape the flesh out of the skin. Or thinly slice through the long cylindrical neck of a butternut squash and roast the slices on high heat as for Harissa-Roasted Squash with Warm Chickpea & Mâche Salad (page 172). You won't even notice the skins, which are actually edible.

Just like pumpkin seeds on Halloween, winter squash seeds can be seasoned, roasted until crunchy, and used to top salads and soups (page 174). The seeds of some varieties of winter squash aren't as delicious as others, as they have very thick shells that don't improve with roasting. Generally butternut squash, popular in soups, is a safe bet, and its seeds can go into the oven at the same time as you roast the squash.

Winter squash can hold for several weeks in a cool, dry place.

HARISSA-ROASTED SQUASH WITH WARM CHICKPEA & MÂCHE SALAD SERVES 4 AS A MAIN COURSE

To cook the chickpeas from scratch, follow the instructions for cooking beans in the Beans & Leek Greens Soup (page 72).

Squash

- 1 small butternut squash (about 1½ pounds; see Note)
- 3 tablespoons olive oil
- ½ teaspoon kosher salt
- 1½ tablespoons harissa, or to taste

Salad

- ½ cup wheat berries soaked overnight (see Note), or farro
- 1½ to 2 cups cooked chickpeas, or 1 (14-ounce) can chickpeas, drained and gently reheated
- ¼ cup chopped flat-leaf parsley
- 3 tablespoons extra virgin olive oil
- 2 tablespoons fresh lemon juice
- Kosher salt and freshly ground pepper
- 3 to 4 ounces mâche, baby arugula, baby spinach, or tatsoi

Though many recipes call for peeling squash, in this recipe, which first ran in the *San Francisco Chronicle*, you just slice the squash, leaving the skin on. After roasting the rounds until golden at high heat, the skin becomes barely noticeable. Though they are a delicious side dish on their own, the hefty slices of harissa-roasted squash also make a great base to vegetarian meals, such as this main-course grain and chickpea salad.

Note: Smaller, oblong butternut squash that are around 1½ pounds are the easiest to work with here, and if they are mostly cylindrical, they will have very few seeds. Wheat berries are usually sold in the bulk section of large supermarkets. Soaking them overnight softens them and makes them cook faster; farro doesn't need soaking and takes only about 18 minutes to cook.

....

To make the squash, preheat the oven to 425°F and line two baking sheets with parchment paper. Place oven racks in the upper and bottom thirds of the oven.

Cut the squash crosswise into ¼-inch-thick slices. When you reach the seed cavity, scoop out the seeds with a large spoon and slice the rest of the squash.

In a large bowl, whisk together the olive oil, salt, and harissa; the mixture should be fairly spicy. Place the squash rounds in the bowl and toss to coat. Arrange the squash in a single layer on the prepared baking sheets and roast until browned, about 10 minutes; flip and roast on the other side until tender, another 10 minutes.

To make the salad, place the wheat berries in a medium pot of salted water and simmer until the beans are tender but still have a crunch, about 40 to 60 minutes or according to package directions. Drain well.

Combine the wheat berries, chickpeas, parsley, olive oil, and lemon juice in a large bowl. Add salt and pepper to taste. Let sit a few minutes to absorb the dressing.

Right before serving, fold in the mâche and adjust the seasoning. Distribute onto 4 plates and top with the squash.

BUTTERNUT SQUASH SOUP WITH TOASTED SEEDS SERVES 6

Use any leftover leek greens in the Leek Greens Stir-Fry with Salty Pork Belly (page 67).

1 teaspoon ground cumin

1 teaspoon kosher salt

½ teaspoon freshly ground pepper

½ teaspoon cinnamon

⅛ teaspoon cayenne pepper

4 pounds butternut squash

1 teaspoon sugar

1 tablespoon unsalted butter or olive oil

1 onion, thinly sliced, or 1 large leek, washed (see Prep Tip, page 64), white and light green parts only

3 cloves garlic, minced

1 tablespoon minced fresh sage (optional)

4 cups Vegetable Scraps Stock (page 10) or other vegetable or chicken broth

¼ cup heavy cream

1 tablespoon fresh lemon juice

Here's a way to use almost the whole squash without missing out on the delicious crunchy seeds inside. Roasting the squash caramelizes the flavor, which is heightened by a spice mixture, resulting in a smooth, luscious soup. Although you leave the skin on in the previous butternut squash recipe, in this one you remove the skin because it would detract from the silkiness of the soup.

....

Preheat the oven to 375°F.

Combine the cumin, salt, pepper, cinnamon, and cayenne in a small bowl.

Cut the squash in half and remove and set aside the seeds. Sprinkle the cavities of the squash with half of the spice mixture and place cut side down on a rimmed baking sheet. Fill the pan with ½ inch of water. Bake until the squash is tender, about 1 hour and 15 minutes. Remove from the oven and let cool, reserving the water. When it is cool enough to handle, scoop the squash flesh into a bowl and add the water. Set aside.

Meanwhile, remove the pulp from the seeds and rinse thoroughly, then measure out ¾ cup of the seeds. Spread the seeds out on a baking sheet lined with a clean kitchen towel or paper towels and let dry for at least 15 minutes. In a medium bowl, toss the seeds with the remaining spice mixture and the sugar. Spread on a greased baking sheet and toast in the oven until crisp, about 15 minutes, stirring once. Let cool.

Heat the butter in a Dutch oven. Add the onion and sauté over medium-low heat, stirring often, until very soft, 10 to 12 minutes. Stir in the garlic and sage, and cook until fragrant, about 1 minute. Add the squash, squash water, and stock. Bring to a simmer and cook until the flavors come together, about 5 minutes. Stir in the cream and lemon juice and heat gently until warmed through (do not let it come to a boil or the cream might curdle).

Use an immersion blender or regular blender to puree the soup, in batches if necessary, until smooth. Season with salt and pepper to taste and serve with the toasted squash seeds.

Citrus

Lemons, limes, oranges, tangerines, and grapefruit provide a little sunshine and color during the winter, when most of our favorite fruits are out of season. While we prize these tangy fruits for their plump segments and juice, their zest is also packed with flavor and fragrant oils.

Citrus rinds usually just get tossed out, but if you have a little extra time, remove the zest with a fine grater before juicing up a bunch of lemons for lemonade or segmenting grapefruit for a salad. After the zest dries on a baking sheet overnight, it lasts for months in a jar and adds an intense flavor and aroma to many dishes, with a little less of the bitterness found in freshly grated zest.

In addition to the recipes that follow, the Herb-Citrus Butter (page 98), the Basil-Lemon Pistou (page 99), the Golden Broccoli Spears with Tangerine Peel (page 130), and the Lemony Watermelon Rind Pickles (page 192) also provide uses for extra zest.

Citrus fruit holds for at least a week in the vegetable drawer of the refrigerator. After zesting, however, the fruit dries out quickly, so wrap zested fruit in plastic bags and use within a day or two.

DRIED CITRUS ZEST MAKES ABOUT 3 TABLESPOONS

2 large organic lemons,
4 limes, 1 orange, or
1 grapefruit

This is the quickest and easiest way I know to preserve citrus zest. Some coordination is required. You have to zest fruit before you cut it up for juicing or salads, but you also have to use the fruit itself soon after zesting, because it no longer has that protective outer layer and dries up quickly. Add some of this zest to vinaigrettes, fruit salads, meat braises, cakes, or anything needing a little citrus boost. Or, use it in the Crispy Lemon Cookies (page 178).

Using a Microplane grater, remove all of the colored part of the zest from the fruit, turning it as you go to reach as much of the zest as possible. Leave behind the white pith. Spread the zest out on a parchment-lined rimmed baking sheet, and separate as many clumps as you can so it dries thoroughly.

Let stand at room temperature until completely dry, at least 4 hours or overnight. As it starts to dry, separate any clumps that are still together.

Store the zest in an airtight container in a cool, dark place for several months at room temperature.

CRISPY LEMON COOKIES MAKES AROUND 75 SMALL COOKIES

- 1½ cups all-purpose flour
- 2 teaspoons baking powder
- ¼ teaspoon kosher salt
- ⅓ cup fresh lemon juice (from 2 lemons)
- 1 teaspoon vanilla extract
- ½ cup granulated sugar
- ½ cup light brown sugar
- 3 tablespoons dried lemon zest (page 177), or 2 tablespoons fresh lemon zest
- ½ cup unsalted butter, at cool room temperature

Something about the dried zest makes these refrigerator cookies especially lemony. Then again, if you don't have dried zest on hand, you can use the fresh zest from the 2 lemons called for in this recipe (zest them before squeezing for juice). After making the dough, you roll it into a log, chill it, and then slice it to bake. For an intriguing orange-flavored, pink version, try substituting blood oranges for the lemons.

....

In a small bowl, combine the flour, baking powder, and salt. Combine the lemon juice and vanilla in a small liquid measuring cup.

Place the sugars and zest in a mixer fitted with the paddle attachment. Mix on medium speed until well incorporated, about 2 minutes. Add the butter and start the mixer on slow speed to incorporate it, then mix on medium speed until the butter is creamed into the sugar, about 3 minutes.

Scrape down the sides of the bowl, and then add some the flour mixture on low speed until just incorporated. Add some of the lemon juice mixture, then mix again briefly. Repeat, alternating between the dry and wet ingredients until all have been added.

Divide the mixture in half, then, on a clean work surface, roll each portion back and forth to make an 18-inch cylinder about 1½ inches in diameter. Wrap the logs in plastic wrap and roll again to make them as round as possible, which will make the cookies rounder. Chill until cold and very firm, at least 2 hours in the refrigerator or 30 minutes in the freezer. (Tightly wrapped, the dough will hold at this point for 5 days in the refrigerator or 2 months in the freezer. To use, let the dough defrost but keep it cool.)

Preheat the oven to 375°F. Line cookie sheets with parchment paper or Silpat mats.

Roll the logs again to make them more uniformly round. Slice the logs into rounds ¼ inch thick and place on the pans, leaving at least 1 inch between cookies. Bake until slightly brown on the edges, 10 to 12 minutes. Let cool in the pan for 5 minutes, then transfer to cooling racks and let cool completely.

Tomatoes

Height-of-summer, perfectly ripe, locally grown tomatoes cause Californians to erupt in religious fervor. Our local farmers grow incredible tomatoes between around the Fourth of July and Halloween, the fruit's holy months and the only time a respectable person can be seen buying them. This is when you can find the psychedelic-colored heirlooms that slice into big, silky wedges and the dry-farmed Early Girls, which are grown without irrigation to produce red orbs packed with concentrated flavor.

Because about 90 percent of a tomato is pure deliciousness, it's not the most wasteful food. But there are a few times where you might find yourself with excess parts, which seem even more valuable after you've handed over $20 for a pile of Green Zebras and Cherokee Purples. If you, like me, can't bear to see the juices and seeds left over from chopping tomatoes go to waste, you can collect them and turn them into a savory granita (page 183). And if you find yourself bingeing when you buy tomatoes at the market, you can always roast the extra ones on low heat and then puree them into Fresh Tomato Paste in Olive Oil (page 181), which is infused with summertime sweetness.

Refrigeration ruins the texture of ripe tomatoes, which should be held at room temperature instead. Place the tomatoes stem side down in a cool, dry place for 1 to 2 days.

Prep Tip

To seed tomatoes, start by cutting the tomato in half crosswise. Then use a small knife or your finger to remove the clusters of seeds and liquid from each pocket inside the tomato.

FRESH TOMATO PASTE
IN OLIVE OIL MAKES ¾ CUP

Use the tomato seeds and water in the Tomato Water–Cucumber Granita (page 183).

When you have extra tomatoes from the farmers' market or garden, you can preserve them using this easy method. First oven-dry them for a few hours or even overnight. When you puree them with olive oil and place the sweet, jammy mixture in a jar, it will hold for at least a month, ready to be stirred into pasta sauces or salad dressings or used as a bruschetta topping with a little sea salt and chopped basil—or whatever else you can dream up. Feel free to use both the paste and the flavorful oil.

Note: It's not necessary to remove the stem ends of the tomatoes, stray seeds, or skins, which you won't notice in the final puree.

1 pound tomatoes, halved crosswise and seeded (see Prep Tip, page 180)

Kosher or sea salt

½ cup extra-virgin olive oil, plus more for topping the jar

Preheat the oven to 250°F.

Grease a baking dish with olive oil or line it with parchment paper. Place the tomatoes in the pan, cut side up, then season with salt. Bake until shrunken and mostly dry, about 3½ hours. (You can continue baking for up to 8 hours, or overnight at the same temperature; the flavor will just get more concentrated.) Let cool.

Puree the tomatoes with the olive oil in a food processor or blender until completely blended, up to 2 minutes. Pour into a jar, tap on the counter to release any air pockets, and top with extra olive oil to cover.

The paste will keep in the refrigerator, tightly covered, for 2 weeks. Always top off with extra olive oil to cover the surface of the paste to prevent mold from forming.

TOMATO WATER–CUCUMBER
GRANITA MAKES 4 SMALL SERVINGS

*Use the cucumbers and
tomatoes in the Radish
Leaf Salad with Corn,
Tomatoes & Salted
Cucumbers (page 29).*

**Seeds, juice, and
scraps from chopping
1½ pounds ripe tomatoes
(see Prep Tip, page 180)**

**Seeds and juice from
1 large cucumber (8 to
10 ounces)**

1 tablespoon sugar

½ teaspoon kosher salt

½ teaspoon sherry vinegar

Pinch of cayenne pepper

Some recipes for tomato-based pasta sauces, salsas, and garden salads call for removing the pockets of seeds from the tomatoes so the focus is on the tomato's meaty flesh. The same is true of cucumbers, which have a core of seeds and juices running through their center that you can remove to prevent salads from getting too watery. But these little clusters of seeds are surrounded by flavorful juices. Instead of throwing them away, strain them to make a small batch of savory, intensely flavored granita for an old-fashioned palate cleanser or refreshing little taste on a hot afternoon.

Note: You'll get more intensely flavored and colored tomato water in the fruit's high season, and the amount of water released by cucumbers and tomatoes will also vary depending on their variety. This recipe is based on the quantity of tomatoes that you might use to make a batch of bruschetta or pasta sauce, so it only makes a demitasse-size serving per person, but you can increase the proportions. An all-tomato version works well, too.

Put the tomato and cucumber seeds and juice in a fine-mesh strainer set over a small bowl. Add any other scraps from chopping, let drain, and then use a spoon to press the seeds and scraps to release more juices. You should end up with between ²/₃ and 1 cup liquid.

Bring ¼ cup water to a boil in a small saucepan on the stove or place the water in a glass measuring pitcher and bring to a boil by heating in the microwave for 30 seconds. Add the sugar and salt, stir to dissolve, and add to the tomato-cucumber water along with the vinegar and cayenne. You can adjust seasoning if needed; it will taste sweet now, but this will dissipate with freezing.

Place the mixture in an 8 by 8-inch glass baking dish and freeze for 30 minutes. Rake with a fork, breaking up any frozen crystals. Continue freezing and scraping every 30 minutes until slushy, about 1½ hours total. (You can hold the granita an hour or two longer in the freezer if you stir it occasionally.) Serve in shot glasses with small spoons.

Prep Tip

The part of the watermelon rind you want to use in recipes is the thin white strip between the dark green skin and the red or yellow fruit. Start with a whole or half watermelon. If whole, cut a thin slice from the top and bottom of the melon and place on either the flat top or bottom. With a firm grasp on a sturdy vegetable peeler, remove the dark green skin in long strokes, then flip the melon to take care of any remaining parts of the peel. Finish by shaving off any remaining traces of dark green, which make the rind fibrous. Cut the watermelon into the size called for in the recipe, then place flat on a cutting board and use a paring knife to remove the white rind from the fruit.

Watermelon

During summer, the prime season for melons, the best specimens tend to be the smaller heirloom varieties. But even small watermelons can weigh 4 or 6 pounds, which can still be a lot of melon to eat without a lawn full of picnicking relatives. Since watermelon turns mealy with too much refrigeration, it's best to eat it quickly after cutting it open.

If I have a lot of leftover watermelon or one that isn't very sweet, I like to turn it into an agua fresca (page 191), the fresh Mexican drink of pureed fruit mixed with cool water and a bit of sugar. You can take it in another direction in a Thai-style salad that harnesses the melon's fruit-punch sweetness with savory, funky flavors like Thai basil, fish sauce, and serrano chiles (page 187). Watermelon rind plays an important role in this salad, a crunchy, slightly sour part of the fruit that absorbs a marinade of lemongrass-infused syrup and lime to play off the juicy chunks of melon. Or you can conjure up more of those picnicking aunties with a fresh, lemony take on watermelon rind pickles (page 192), the crunchy, translucent condiment made from the part of the fruit that usually goes in the trash.

Store whole melons in a cool, dry place for a few days and chill only right before serving.

THAI WATERMELON SALAD WITH CRUNCHY WATERMELON RIND SERVES 6

Use the rest of the lemongrass in the Lemongrass Grilled Chicken (page 109), which is a great partner to this salad.

Lemongrass syrup

- ½ **cup sugar**
- ½ **cup water**
- ½ **cup lemongrass, cut in 1-inch pieces, from the tops of 4 stalks**

Salad

- 3 **pounds seedless watermelon, unpeeled**
- 3 **tablespoons lime juice (from 2 to 3 juicy limes)**
- 1 **tablespoon plus 1 teaspoon Asian fish sauce**
- 2 **tablespoons thinly sliced shallot**
- 2 **tablespoons thinly sliced basil, preferably Thai basil**
- 1 **serrano chile, chopped**
- 2 **to 4 cups mâche or baby spinach (optional)**

Here is an unexpected use for that half of a watermelon you're not sure what to do with. With a flavor profile similar to that of Thai green papaya or banana blossom salad, this recipe takes advantage of crisp, refreshing watermelon rind, which is marinated in a mixture of lemongrass syrup, lime juice, basil, fresh chiles, and fish sauce. After the rind has absorbed all the flavors, you toss it with cubes of fresh watermelon for a juicy dish that I find difficult to stop eating, as the sweet watermelon plays against the savory, spicy, and tart flavors. If you can find mâche, a tender dark green lettuce, it adds beautiful contrasting color and even more juicy crunch to the combination.

Note: Most recipes that call for lemongrass only use the bulbous bottom parts, but here you can use the leftover top part of the stalks, or use 2 whole lemongrass stalks. You will have some leftover syrup, which is delicious in cocktails, lemonade, or desserts (see Fruit and Herbal Syrups, Chunky & Clear, page 189).

To make the lemongrass syrup, place the sugar and water in a small saucepan over medium heat. Cook, stirring, until the sugar dissolves, 2 to 3 minutes. Add the lemongrass stalks, return to a simmer, and cook until the lemongrass flavor is infused into the syrup, 5 to 7 minutes. Let cool, then strain.

To make the salad, remove the white rind from the watermelon (see Prep Tip, page 185). Chop the melon flesh into ¾-inch cubes (you should have around 4 cups) and refrigerate until serving. Cut the rind into julienne until you have 2 cups. Place in a small bowl and add 2 tablespoons of the lemongrass syrup, 2 tablespoons of the lime juice, 1 tablespoon of the fish sauce, the shallot, the basil, and half of the serrano. Toss to combine, then cover and marinate, refrigerated, for 1 to 3 hours.

To serve, place the cold watermelon cubes in a large bowl and cover with the marinated rind and its juices. Season with the remaining 1 tablespoon lime juice, the remaining 1 teaspoon fish sauce, and the remaining serrano pepper (or to taste). Add the mâche and gently toss. Serve immediately while still very cold.

Fruit & Herbal Syrups, Chunky & Clear

Making a syrup is one of the easiest ways to preserve fruits and herbs. There are two types: clear simple syrups, in which you infuse herbs or parts of vegetables or fruits into a combination of equal parts sugar and water and then strain it, and chunky syrups, when you cook fresh fruit, usually berries, with a small amount of sugar and water to make a topping for yogurt, oatmeal, waffles, or desserts.

Simple syrups are used in baking and making beverages, and using fruit- or herb-flavored varieties adds interest to a basic cake, sparkling lemonade, classic cocktail, or even salad dressing. This book includes two examples of infused simple syrup: the lemongrass-infused simple syrup used for the Thai Watermelon Salad with Crunchy Watermelon Rind (page 187) and fennel syrup in the recipe for Candied Fennel Stalk (page 63). Use the technique described in the lemongrass syrup recipe—using roughly the same proportions of sugar, water, and coarsely chopped herbs, citrus peels, or vegetable extras—to make other versions with unexpected flavors such as rosemary, celery, ginger, or grapefruit. Brush the syrup over cake layers before frosting them, or pour some into a glass with equal parts lemon or lime juice and plenty of still or sparkling water for a refreshing drink.

To make a chunky fruit syrup, use 2 tablespoons sugar and 2 tablespoons water for every cup of chopped stone fruit or berries. Place in a saucepan and simmer until the fruit has released its juices and is softened to the texture you like, 5 to 10 minutes. (Denser fruit like apples and pears take more like 20 minutes to soften.) You could add citrus zest or whole spices, such as cinnamon sticks, during cooking, and add lemon juice and more sugar to taste when it's done. You can also substitute maple syrup and brown sugar for white sugar. The chunky syrup will hold for 1 week or longer, depending on the acidity of the fruit.

WATERMELON AGUA FRESCA SERVES 6 TO 8

Use the watermelon rind in the Lemony Water-melon Rind Pickles (page 192).

4 pounds seedless watermelon

4 cups cold water

Juice of 1 to 2 limes

2 to 3 tablespoons sugar

⅛ teaspoon kosher salt

Take a tip from your neighborhood taqueria, and use up half a watermelon left from a party or barbecue in a fruity "water," or Mexican agua fresca. Adjust the amount of sugar and lime juice to the sweetness of the fruit and to your own taste. This recipe works equally well with cantaloupe and other melons; I often use it to perk up melons that turn out to be disappointingly bland or underripe.

Note: If you are feeling creative, you can use an infused simple syrup instead of sugar, such as one made with ginger or lime zest (see Fruit & Herbal Syrups, page 189). You'll need around ¼ cup syrup; just add it to taste.

Peel the watermelon (see Prep Tip, page 185) and cut the flesh into 1-inch chunks. Place the watermelon chunks, water, the juice of 1 lime, 2 tablespoons sugar, and the salt in a blender and puree until smooth. Taste and adjust the amount of sugar and lime, if necessary. Pour into a pitcher and serve over ice.

LEMONY WATERMELON RIND PICKLES MAKES 2 TO 3 PINTS

Rind from 3 pounds
seedless watermelon
(see Prep Tip, page 185)

7 cups water

5 tablespoons kosher salt

⅔ cup sugar

1 cup apple cider vinegar

1 cinnamon stick, broken
in half

½ teaspoon peppercorns

½ teaspoon whole cloves

Zest (in large strips) and
juice from 1 large lemon

Most watermelon rind pickles, an old-fashioned treat, are very sweet. I dialed back the sugar a bit to make a tart-sweet pickle with a prominent lemon flavor. On the salty side, these remind me of a juicy version of Moroccan preserved lemons. Serve a plate of watermelon pickles with grilled meats or sandwiches, or finely dice them into a tuna salad.

Note: You will need 2 or 3 pint jars and canning lids and rings, cleaned well in soapy water. Because this doesn't make a huge amount, you can store it in the refrigerator for 1 to 2 months rather than canning it. You may have some extra brine, so feel free to add more rind if you have it.

Cut the rind into 1-inch cubes to make around 4 cups.

Combine 6 cups of the water and 3 tablespoons of the salt in a large saucepan. Bring to a simmer to dissolve the salt, then add the watermelon rind and cook until fork tender, about 8 minutes. Drain the watermelon rind and divide among the pint jars.

In a small saucepan, combine the remaining 1 cup water with the remaining 2 tablespoons salt, the sugar, vinegar, cinnamon stick, peppercorns, and cloves. Bring to a simmer, stirring until the sugar and salt have dissolved.

Stir the lemon zest and juice into the pickle brine. Pour the brine over the watermelon rind, distributing the spices and lemon zest evenly among the jars. Let cool, then cover and refrigerate overnight before serving. (The pickles will taste very salty at first, but the flavor mellows overnight.)

The pickles will keep for 1 month, refrigerated.

RECIPES BY TYPE

APPETIZERS

- Fontina-Stuffed Squash Blossom Fritters **125**
- Green Ceviche **106**
- Leek Greens & Shrimp Pot Stickers **68**
- Potato Skin–Bacon Fat Chips **38**
- Roasted Artichoke Leaves **123**
- Scraps Latkes **40**
- Tomato Water–Cucumber Granita **183**
- Whole Grilled Favas **151**

SIDE DISHES

- Braised Turnips & Greens with Soy Butter **26**
- Broiled Cauliflower Steaks with Mustard Glaze **139**
- Carrot Top Salsa Verde with Roasted Root Vegetables **34**
- Chard Stalk Hummus **91**
- Corn-Pancetta Puddings in Corn Husk Baskets **147**
- Garlic-Braised Greens **87**
- Golden Broccoli Spears with Tangerine Peel **130**
- Pan-Roasted Cauliflower Steaks with Tomatoes & Capers **135**
- Pea Pod Pudding **153**

SOUPS & STOCKS

- Asparagus Stalk Stock **47**
- Beans & Leek Greens Soup **72**
- Butternut Squash Soup with Toasted Seeds **174**
- Creamy Asparagus & Celery Heart Soup with Tarragon **50**
- Romaine Leaf Soup with Leeks & Peas **114**
- Smoky Corn Cob Chowder **145**
- Vegetable Scraps Stock **10**

SALADS

- Beet Greens Salad with Whole Grains, Pickled Beets & Fresh Cheese **20**
- Carrot Slaw with Greek Yogurt, Lemon & Coriander **31**
- Celery Slaw with Apple Peel & Ginger Dressing **52**
- Fattoush Salad **110**
- Fennel Parmesan Salad **55**
- Gialina's Kale & Farro Salad with Avocado **92**
- Harissa-Roasted Squash with Warm Chickpea & Mâche Salad **172**
- Quinoa-Carrot Tabbouleh **36**
- Radish Leaf Salad with Corn, Tomatoes & Salted Cucumbers **29**
- Shaved Broccoli Stalk Salad with Lime & Cotija **129**
- Thai Watermelon Salad with Crunchy Watermelon Rind **187**

MAIN COURSES

- Asparagus, Artichoke & Chickpea Ragout **49**
- Beet Greens Strata **23**
- Broccoli Stalk Orecchiette with Anchovies & Garlic Bread Crumbs **131**
- Cabbage Rolls with Ginger Pork **80**
- Cauliflower with Smoked Paprika & Whole Wheat Linguine **136**
- Chilaquiles with Cilantro Salsa & Queso Fresco **105**
- Fennel-Braised Pork Roast **61**
- Fennel-Roasted Whole Fish with Potatoes **58**
- Leek Greens Stir-Fry with Salty Pork Belly **67**
- Lemongrass Grilled Chicken **109**
- Romaine Wraps with Brown Rice & Bulgogi **116**
- Salmon with Whole Grilled Lettuce & Charred Tomatoes **115**
- Steamed Mussels with Celery Leaf Salad **53**

CONDIMENTS, SAUCES & PICKLES

- Apple-Wine Jelly **163**
- Avocado-Lemon Dressing with Toasted Cumin **170**
- Basil-Lemon Pistou **99**
- Chard Stalk Relish with Pine Nuts & Sultanas **89**
- Chimichurri **102**
- Cilantro Chutney **103**
- Cilantro Salsa **108**
- Crispy Fried Leek Greens **65**
- Dried Citrus Zest **177**
- Fresh Tomato Paste in Olive Oil **181**
- Fruit & Herbal Syrups, Chunky & Clear **189**
- Herb-Citrus Butter **98**
- Herb Salt **96**
- Lemony Watermelon Rind Pickles **192**
- Rosemary Lard Butter **100**
- Sauerkraut **83**

DESSERTS

- Candied Fennel Stalk & Fennel Syrup **63**
- Crispy Lemon Cookies **178**
- Extra-Fruit Crisp **161**

BEVERAGES

- Apple Peel Bourbon **164**
- Apple-Wine "Jus" & Jelly **163**
- Avocado Lassi **169**
- Watermelon Agua Fresca **191**

ACKNOWLEDGMENTS

I would first like to thank the wonderful team at Ten Speed publishing, especially Aaron Wehner, Betsy Stromberg, Katy Brown, Kelly Snowden, and the always gracious and insightful Melissa Moore, the editor of this book.

My agent, Danielle Svetcov, had the idea for this book after seeing an article I wrote in the *San Francisco Chronicle,* and now she has helped make it happen.

Thanks to Clay McLachlan for his beautiful photography and for always being so dedicated and full of ideas. Thanks go to Caitlin Freeman for photo styling, hosting the photo shoot, sending recipe testers my way, and her overall good advice.

Sharron Wood is the talented wordsmith who copyedited this book, and my constant cocktail consultant. Tim Dolan kindly provided legal counsel, and Molly Watson offered editorial counsel over rounds of matzo brei.

Thanks so much to the chefs who shared recipes and ideas: Sharon Ardiana, Luke and Tony Sung, Kathryn Lukas, Paula Wolfert, Daniel Patterson, Bruce Hill, Laurence Jossel, Peter McNee, Amanda Gold, Marla Simon, and Alice Medrich in particular, who also taught me a lot about chocolate.

I am indebted to my vegetable-parts braving recipe testers: Michelle Arkin, Joanne Bedwell, Tammy Cooke, Frances Culp, Jean Debroux, Alyssa Meijer Drees, Jane Duggan (thanks, Mom!), Gordon Edgar, Kathy Ems, Caitlin Freeman, Brigid Gaffikin, Michele Garcia, Kristina Hallett, Tilde Herrera, Alexandra Holbrook, Julie Jares, Seton Mangine, Alicia Penzel, Imelda Punsalan, Arijana Rakich, Karen Reardanz, Elisabeth Schriber (and her rabbit), Amy Shelf, and Joanne Sy.

At the main photo shoot, Stuart Brioza and Nicole Krasinski loaned their stunning handmade plates, Carrie Goldberg provided cooking assistance, and Dylan McLachlan filmed the process.

At the *San Francisco Chronicle* Food & Wine department, I am lucky to work with an incredible group of people who always inform what I do: Michael Bauer, Jon Bonné, Lynne Char Bennett, Stacy Finz, Sarah Fritsche, Amanda Gold, Janny Hu, Craig Lee, Paolo Lucchesi, Allen Matthews, Miriam Morgan, Deb Wandell, Jillian Welsch, and Erick Wong. I also appreciate the many *Chronicle* readers who send me questions, and keep me on my toes.

Ben Duggan and Jennifer Ketring's dedication to the art of vegetable growing has taught me so much, and I'm grateful for the love and support of the rest of my clan and friends: Mom and Dad, Logan, Bryce, Dee, Mark, Mary, Dave, and Olivia, plus Sharron, Michelle, Bip, Janna Cordeiro, Nora Dolan, Rachael Myrow, and Terri Wu.

Mostly, I wouldn't be anywhere without my family, Eric, Dahlia, and Elsie.

ABOUT THE AUTHOR

TARA DUGGAN is a staff writer for *The San Francisco Chronicle*'s Food & Wine section and the author of three previous cookbooks, including *The Blue Bottle Craft of Coffee* and *The Working Cook*. A graduate of the California Culinary Academy, she is the recipient of a James Beard Foundation Journalism Award. Her writing has appeared in *The New York Times*, *The Denver Post*, *The Chicago Tribune*, and *The Toronto Star*. Tara, her husband, and their two daughters live in San Francisco and enjoy spending time on her family's off-the-grid farm in Northern California, where she gets ideas for what to do with all kinds of kitchen scraps.

INDEX

For a list of recipes by type, please see pages 193–94.

A

Agua Fresca,
    Watermelon, 191
Apples, 160
    Apple Peel Bourbon, 164
    Apple-Wine "Jus" &
      Jelly, 163
    Celery Slaw with Apple Peel
      & Ginger Dressing, 52
    Extra-Fruit Crisp, 161–62
Artichokes, 122
    Asparagus, Artichoke &
      Chickpea Ragout, 49
    Roasted Artichoke
      Leaves, 123
Asparagus, 46
    Asparagus, Artichoke &
      Chickpea Ragout, 49
    Asparagus Stalk Stock, 47
    Creamy Asparagus &
      Celery Heart Soup with
      Tarragon, 50
Avocados, 168
    Avocado Lassi, 169
    Avocado-Lemon Dressing
      with Toasted Cumin, 170
    Gialina's Kale & Farro
      Salad with Avocado,
      92–94

B

Basil-Lemon Pistou, 99
Beans
    Beans & Leek Greens Soup,
      72–73
    See also Chickpeas; Fava
      beans

Beef
    Romaine Wraps with
      Brown Rice & Bulgogi,
      116–17
Beets, 18
    Beet Greens Salad with
      Whole Grains, Pickled
      Beets & Fresh Cheese,
      20–21
    Beet Greens Strata, 23–24
    Scraps Latkes, 40
Bourbon, Apple Peel, 164
Broccoli, 127
    Broccoli Stalk Orecchiette
      with Anchovies & Garlic
      Bread Crumbs, 131–32
    Golden Broccoli Spears
      with Tangerine Peel, 130
    Shaved Broccoli Stalk
      Salad with Lime &
      Cotija, 129
Bulgogi, Romaine Wraps
    with Brown Rice &,
    116–17
Butter
    Herb-Citrus Butter, 98
    Rosemary Lard Butter,
      100–101
Butternut squash, 171
    Butternut Squash Soup
      with Toasted Seeds,
      174–75
    Harissa-Roasted Squash
      with Warm Chickpea &
      Mâche Salad, 172–73

C

Cabbage, 78
    Cabbage Rolls with Ginger
      Pork, 80–81
    Celery Slaw with
      Apple Peel & Ginger
      Dressing, 52
    Sauerkraut, 83–84
Carrots, 30
    Carrot Slaw with Greek
      Yogurt, Lemon &
      Coriander, 31
    Carrot Top Salsa Verde
      with Roasted Root
      Vegetables, 34–35
    Quinoa-Carrot
      Tabbouleh, 36
    Scraps Latkes, 40
Cauliflower, 133
    Broiled Cauliflower Steaks
      with Mustard Glaze, 139
    Cauliflower with Smoked
      Paprika & Whole Wheat
      Linguine, 136–38
    Pan-Roasted Cauliflower
      Steaks with Tomatoes &
      Capers, 135
Celery, 51
    Celery Slaw with
      Apple Peel & Ginger
      Dressing, 52
    Creamy Asparagus &
      Celery Heart Soup with
      Tarragon, 50
    Steamed Mussels with
      Celery Leaf Salad, 53

Ceviche, Green, 106
Chard, 85–86
  Chard Stalk Hummus, 91
  Chard Stalk Relish with
    Pine Nuts & Sultanas,
    89–90
  Garlic-Braised Greens, 87
Cheese
  Beet Greens Salad with
    Whole Grains, Pickled
    Beets & Fresh Cheese,
    20–21
  Beet Greens Strata, 23–24
  Cauliflower with Smoked
    Paprika & Whole Wheat
    Linguine, 136–38
  Chilaquiles with Cilantro
    Salsa & Queso Fresco, 105
  Fattoush Salad, 110–12
  Fennel Parmesan Salad, 55
  Fontina-Stuffed Squash
    Blossom Fritters, 125–26
  Shaved Broccoli Stalk Salad
    with Lime & Cotija, 129
Chicken, Lemongrass
    Grilled, 109
Chickpeas
  Asparagus, Artichoke &
    Chickpea Ragout, 49
  Harissa-Roasted Squash
    with Warm Chickpea &
    Mâche Salad, 172–73
Chilaquiles with Cilantro
    Salsa & Queso Fresco, 105
Chimichurri, 102
Chutney, Cilantro, 103
Cilantro
  Chilaquiles with Cilantro
    Salsa & Queso Fresco, 105
  Cilantro Chutney, 103
  Cilantro Salsa, 108
  Green Ceviche, 106
Cookies, Crispy Lemon,
    178–79

Corn, 144
  Corn-Pancetta Puddings
    in Corn Husk Baskets,
    147–48
  Radish Leaf Salad with
    Corn, Tomatoes & Salted
    Cucumbers, 29
  Smoky Corn Cob
    Chowder, 145
Crisp, Extra-Fruit, 161–62
Cucumbers
  Fattoush Salad, 110–12
  Quinoa-Carrot
    Tabbouleh, 36
  Radish Leaf Salad with
    Corn, Tomatoes & Salted
    Cucumbers, 29
  Romaine Wraps with
    Brown Rice & Bulgogi,
    116–17
  Tomato Water–Cucumber
    Granita, 183–84

D

Dressing, Avocado-Lemon,
    with Toasted Cumin, 170

F

Farro
  Gialina's Kale & Farro
    Salad with Avocado,
    92–94
  Harissa-Roasted Squash
    with Warm Chickpea &
    Mâche Salad, 172–73
Fattoush Salad, 110–12
Fava beans, 149
  Whole Grilled Favas, 151
Fennel, 54
  Candied Fennel Stalk &
    Fennel Syrup, 63
  Fennel-Braised Pork Roast,
    61–62
  Fennel Parmesan Salad, 55

Fennel-Roasted Whole
    Fish with Potatoes, 58–60
Fish
  Broccoli Stalk Orecchiette
    with Anchovies & Garlic
    Bread Crumbs, 131–32
  Fennel-Roasted Whole
    Fish with Potatoes, 58–60
  filleting, 60
  Green Ceviche, 106
  Salmon with Whole
    Grilled Lettuce &
    Charred Tomatoes, 115
Fritters, Fontina-Stuffed
    Squash Blossom, 125–26
Fruits
  Extra-Fruit Crisp, 161–62
  organic, 7
  syrups, 189
  See also individual fruits

G

Garlic-Braised Greens, 87
Granita, Tomato Water–
    Cucumber, 183–84
Grapefruit, 176
  Dried Citrus Zest, 177
  Herb-Citrus Butter, 98

H

Harissa-Roasted Squash
    with Warm Chickpea &
    Mâche Salad, 172–73
Herbs, 95
  Herb-Citrus Butter, 98
  Herb Salt, 96
  syrups, 189
  See also individual herbs
Hummus, Chard Stalk, 91

J

Jelly, Apple-Wine, 163

K

Kale, 85–86
  Garlic-Braised Greens, 87
  Gialina's Kale & Farro
    Salad with Avocado,
    92–94

L

Lard Butter, Rosemary,
  100–101
Lassi, Avocado, 169
Latkes, Scraps, 40
Leeks, 64
  Asparagus Stalk Stock, 47
  Beans & Leek Greens Soup,
    72–73
  Beet Greens Strata, 23–24
  Braised Turnips & Greens
    with Soy Butter, 26–27
  Crispy Fried Leek
    Greens, 65
  Fennel-Braised Pork Roast,
    61–62
  Leek Greens & Shrimp Pot
    Stickers, 68–71
  Leek Greens Stir-Fry with
    Salty Pork Belly, 67
  Romaine Leaf Soup with
    Leeks & Peas, 114
  Steamed Mussels with
    Celery Leaf Salad, 53
Lemongrass
  Lemongrass Grilled
    Chicken, 109
  Lemongrass Syrup, 187
  trimming, 109
Lemons, 176
  Avocado-Lemon Dressing
    with Toasted Cumin, 170
  Basil-Lemon Pistou, 99
  Crispy Lemon Cookies,
    178–79
  Dried Citrus Zest, 177
  Herb-Citrus Butter, 98

Lemony Watermelon Rind
  Pickles, 192
Limes, 176
  Dried Citrus Zest, 177
  Green Ceviche, 106
  Herb-Citrus Butter, 98

M

Mussels, Steamed, with
  Celery Leaf Salad, 53

O

Oranges, 176
  Dried Citrus Zest, 177

P

Pancetta
  Corn-Pancetta Puddings
    in Corn Husk Baskets,
    147–48
  Leek Greens Stir-Fry with
    Salty Pork Belly, 67
Parsley
  Chimichurri, 102
Parsnips
  Carrot Top Salsa Verde
    with Roasted Root
    Vegetables, 34–35
  Scraps Latkes, 40
Pasta
  Broccoli Stalk Orecchiette
    with Anchovies & Garlic
    Bread Crumbs, 131–32
  Cauliflower with Smoked
    Paprika & Whole Wheat
    Linguine, 136–38
Peas, 152
  Pea Pod Pudding, 153–54
  Romaine Leaf Soup with
    Leeks & Peas, 114
Pesticides, 7
Pickles, Lemony Watermelon
  Rind, 192
Pistou, Basil-Lemon, 99

Pork
  Cabbage Rolls with Ginger
    Pork, 80–81
  Fennel-Braised Pork Roast,
    61–62
  Leek Greens Stir-Fry with
    Salty Pork Belly, 67
  See also Pancetta
Potatoes, 37
  Carrot Top Salsa Verde
    with Roasted Root
    Vegetables, 34–35
  Creamy Asparagus &
    Celery Heart Soup with
    Tarragon, 50
  Fennel-Roasted Whole
    Fish with Potatoes, 58–60
  Potato Skin–Bacon Fat
    Chips, 38
  Scraps Latkes, 40
  Smoky Corn Cob
    Chowder, 145
Pot Stickers, Leek Greens &
  Shrimp, 68–71
Puddings
  Corn-Pancetta Puddings
    in Corn Husk Baskets,
    147–48
  Pea Pod Pudding, 153–54

Q

Quinoa
  Beet Greens Salad with
    Whole Grains, Pickled
    Beets & Fresh Cheese,
    20–21
  Quinoa-Carrot
    Tabbouleh, 36

R

Radishes, 18
  Radish Leaf Salad with
    Corn, Tomatoes & Salted
    Cucumbers, 29

Relish, Chard Stalk, with
     Pine Nuts & Sultanas,
     89–90
Rice
     Cabbage Rolls with Ginger
         Pork, 80–81
     Romaine Wraps with
         Brown Rice & Bulgogi,
         116–17
Romaine lettuce, 113
     Fattoush Salad, 110–12
     Romaine Leaf Soup with
         Leeks & Peas, 114
     Romaine Wraps with
         Brown Rice & Bulgogi,
         116–17
     Salmon with Whole
         Grilled Lettuce &
         Charred Tomatoes, 115
Rosemary Lard Butter,
     100–101

S
Salsas
     Carrot Top Salsa Verde,
         34–35
     Cilantro Salsa, 108
Salt, Herb, 96
Sauerkraut, 83–84
Scraps Latkes, 40
Shrimp Pot Stickers, Leek
     Greens &, 68–71
Squash. *See* Butternut squash;
     Squash blossoms
Squash blossoms, 124
     Fontina-Stuffed Squash
         Blossom Fritters, 125–26
Strata, Beet Greens, 23–24
Syrups
     chunky fruit, 189
     clear simple, 189
     Fennel Syrup, 63
     Lemongrass Syrup, 187

T
Tabbouleh, Quinoa-Carrot, 36
Tangerines, 176
     Golden Broccoli Spears
         with Tangerine Peel, 130
Thai Watermelon Salad with
     Crunchy Watermelon
     Rind, 187–88
Tomatillos
     Cilantro Salsa, 108
Tomatoes, 180
     Cauliflower with Smoked
         Paprika & Whole Wheat
         Linguine, 136–38
     Corn-Pancetta Puddings
         in Corn Husk Baskets,
         147–48
     Fattoush Salad, 110–12
     Fresh Tomato Paste in
         Olive Oil, 181
     Pan-Roasted Cauliflower
         Steaks with Tomatoes &
         Capers, 135
     Quinoa-Carrot
         Tabbouleh, 36
     Radish Leaf Salad with
         Corn, Tomatoes & Salted
         Cucumbers, 29
     Salmon with Whole
         Grilled Lettuce &
         Charred Tomatoes, 115
     Tomato Water–Cucumber
         Granita, 183–84
Tortillas
     Chilaquiles with Cilantro
         Salsa & Queso Fresco, 105
Turnips, 18
     Braised Turnips & Greens
         with Soy Butter, 26–27
     Carrot Top Salsa Verde
         with Roasted Root
         Vegetables, 34–35
     Scraps Latkes, 40

V
Vegetables
     anatomy of, 12, 13
     Carrot Top Salsa Verde
         with Roasted Root
         Vegetables, 34–35
     organic, 7
     Scraps Latkes, 40
     Vegetable Scraps Stock,
         10–11
     See also individual vegetables

W
Waste, reducing, 8
Watermelon, 185
     Lemony Watermelon Rind
         Pickles, 192
     Thai Watermelon
         Salad with Crunchy
         Watermelon Rind,
         187–88
     Watermelon Agua
         Fresca, 191

Z
Zest, Dried Citrus, 177

The recipe Harissa-Roasted Squash with Warm Chickpea & Mâche Salad was
adapted from the recipe as it was originally published in the *San Francisco Chronicle*.

Library of Congress Cataloging-in-Publication Data

Duggan, Tara.
  Root-to-stalk cooking : the art of using the whole vegetable / Tara Duggan ;
photography by Clay McLachlan. — First edition.
    pages cm
  Includes index.
1. Cooking (Vegetables) I. McLachlan, Clay. II. Title.
  TX801.D85 2013
  641.6'5—dc23

Trade Paperback ISBN: 978-1-60774-412-2
eBook ISBN: 978-1-60774-413-9

Printed in China

Design by Katy Brown
Food and prop styling by Caitlin Freeman, Clay McLachlan, and Tara Duggan

10 9 8 7 6 5 4 3 2 1

First Edition